T0323585

Cambridge Elements ☰

Elements in Magic
edited by
William Pooley
University of Bristol

LOWCOUNTRY CONJURE MAGIC

Historical Archaeology on a Plantation Slave Quarter

Sharon K. Moses
Northern Arizona University

Shaftesbury Road, Cambridge CB2 8EA, United Kingdom

One Liberty Plaza, 20th Floor, New York, NY 10006, USA

477 Williamstown Road, Port Melbourne, VIC 3207, Australia

314–321, 3rd Floor, Plot 3, Splendor Forum, Jasola District Centre,
New Delhi – 110025, India

103 Penang Road, #05–06/07, Visioncrest Commercial, Singapore 238467

Cambridge University Press is part of Cambridge University Press & Assessment,
a department of the University of Cambridge.

We share the University's mission to contribute to society through the pursuit
of education, learning and research at the highest international levels of excellence.

www.cambridge.org
Information on this title: www.cambridge.org/9781009539395

DOI: 10.1017/9781009378406

First published 2024

A catalogue record for this publication is available from the British Library

ISBN 978-1-009-53939-5 Hardback
ISBN 978-1-009-37842-0 Paperback
ISSN 2732-4087 (online)
ISSN 2732-4079 (print)

Cambridge University Press & Assessment has no responsibility for the persistence or
accuracy of URLs for external or third-party internet websites referred to in this
publication and does not guarantee that any content on such websites is, or will
remain, accurate or appropriate.

Lowcountry Conjure Magic

Historical Archaeology on a Plantation Slave Quarter

Elements in Magic

DOI: 10.1017/9781009378406

First published online: December 2024

Sharon K. Moses

Northern Arizona University

Author for correspondence: Sharon K. Moses, sharon.moses@nau.edu

Abstract: Cat Island, South Carolina, was once the location of slave trade activities, including capture of Native Americans for export and the rise of plantations in the Lowcountry for indigo and rice production, from the sixteenth to mid-nineteenth centuries. This Element examines the Hume Plantation Slave Street Project led by the author, and archaeological evidence for hoodoo magic and ritual practices involving "white magic" spells used for protection and treatments for illness and injury, and, alternately, for "black magic," in spells used to exact harm or to kill. This Element is intended as a contribution to the collective knowledge about hoodoo magic practices in the Lowcountry, centered on the Hume Plantation grounds during this period of American history. It is an attempt to examine how attitudes and practices may have changed over time and concludes with a look at select contemporary hoodoo activities conducted in local cemeteries.

Keywords: nkisi, slavery, rootmen, hoodoo, ritual

ISBNs: 9781009539395 (HB), 9781009378420 (PB), 9781009378406 (OC)

ISSNs: 2732-4087 (online), 2732-4079 (print)

Contents

1 Introduction

The Hume Plantation is located on Cat Island, South Carolina in the southeastern United States (see Figure 1) and is the site of the archaeological excavations and findings that are the subject of this Element. Cat Island is one of three islands that today make up the Tom Yawkey Wildlife Center, situated around Winyah Bay (see Figure 2). This Element is based upon a work of historical archaeology and will, therefore, include historical and environmental background information to provide context. The interpretations of ritual activities are based on a combination of that context with archaeological evidence and methods for a holistic understanding.

Historical archaeology has the benefit of archival records and other documentation from which to draw understanding about the historical times in which the research and site are located, but that is only a starting point. As the adage dictates, "history is written by the victor," in this case the dominant members of society: the plantation owners and the white population. Historical literature does not always reveal the whole truth or have the capability to reflect the lived experiences of those whose voices it did not count. Archaeological material can provide a new avenue of understanding not revealed in the written word and sometimes it challenges accepted historical versions of events and everyday life. For these reasons, sources consulted include oral histories and narratives from former slaves and their descendants and accounts from the Works Progress Administration (WPA) and the Federal Writers' Project (FWP) of interviews conducted in the 1930s, newspaper accounts that reflect biases and values, and some personal insights provided in contemporary times by descendants of the enslaved from Cat Island. It is hoped that this Element will contribute insights about the role of ritual and magic in the lives of the enslaved.

Throughout this journey, the enslaved held steadfast to magic performances that provided a sense of control in a world otherwise beyond their control. We will look at the archaeological evidence of some of these magic practices known as *hoodoo*.

Historical archaeological projects are predicated upon an investigator's research questions and so, too, was this Hume Plantation Slave Street Project. Research questions help to define the location and the excavation strategy, and provide the framework for expenditure of resources, time, and effort toward specific goals. Outcomes are wherever the archaeological evidence may lead. Without such a framework, there is a danger of straying from the intended research goals or catering to preconceived biases or accounts. Adaptational or contradictory actions that do not match the historical account are a contribution to knowledge about a targeted period or place in human history. Therefore, the

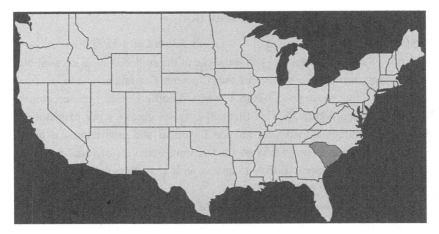

Figure 1 Map of the USA showing South Carolina.
Source: Illustration by the author.

written history and generally accepted truths cannot be applied universally to override what the material evidence presents. Historical archaeology allows both the dominant and the marginalized to be heard based upon *the evidence of their own behaviors* and not necessarily what has been written about them.

Research questions for this project were: (1) What were the hoodoo activities of the enslaved while on their "own time" on the slave street? (2) Can we discern and recognize differences in ritual and magic practices from daily tasks and discard activity in the archaeological record? (3) What hoodoo activities continued in secrecy post-emancipation, or did they revert to practicing openly once the yoke of slavery was removed?

The goals of the Hume Plantation Slave Street Project were to answer questions about the "private" lives of the enslaved and their belief systems and activities. "Private lives" is a phrase used here to describe time away from imposed labor and tasks, understanding that privacy itself was not free of the plantation owner's control. In fact, privacy was fractured within and without the slave cabin in imposed spatial and social restrictions and under the constant watch of the overseer. Stolen moments for hoodoo practice are, therefore, that much more important for understanding the enslaved and meaning in their spiritual lives.

Native American presence and African enslaved populations at this site can be detected from the 17th century onward. By the late 19th century, the Hume Plantation was no more, but descendant community members still resided on or near former plantation grounds into the 20th century.

Hoodoo practices changed over time to address changing needs and were influenced by interactions with other cultures and peoples. Literature on

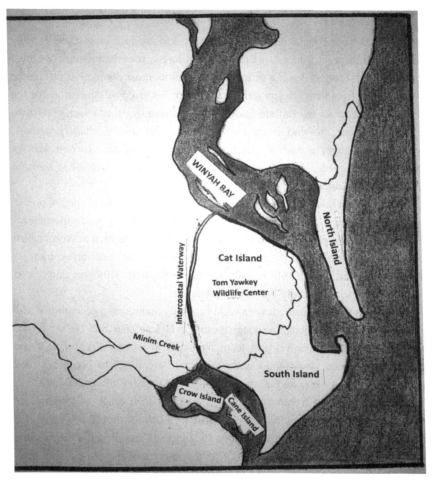

Figure 2 Winyah Bay, South Carolina and the Tom Yawkey Wildlife Center.
Source: Illustration by the author.

African religions has historically taken the approach that the enslaved practiced resistance while quietly preserving their traditions (Chireau 1997; Creel 1988; Jacobs 1987; Klingelhofer 1987; Rucker 2006; Russell 1997; Wilkie 2000; Wood 1974). The Hume Plantation Slave Street Project departed from that premise in that it sought evidence of adaptations that evolved into something new. This is not to say that resistance was not practiced. However, this study's questions seek more than evidence of resistance; they seek evidence of adaptation and cultural synthesis that answered their needs as enslaved people. This would be reflected in ritual and magic activities in their "private lives."

1.1 Hoodoo Defined

Hoodoo has been considered in the realm of African folk magic and *conjure systems* and its practitioners are known as conjurers, root doctors, or root men/ root women. Hoodoo is *not* a religion, which is its most distinctive difference from other African magical practices and often a source of confusion for the public, which tends to conflate hoodoo with Vodun or other specific African religions. Rather, hoodoo is an *unstructured collection of ritual practices, prayers, magic spells, and objects that, when combined in a certain way by those knowledgeable, are believed to bring about results not obtained through human action alone.*

Conjurers/root doctors are individuals that are believed to have special power to call upon Nature, ancestral spirits, and other entities to harness supernatural power to their own purpose. Historically, conjurers could be men or women but, according to some Hume Plantation descendant families' memories, hoodoo practitioners there in the 19th century tended to be men. This was due not to a patriarchal social structure but to circumstance.

Conjuring is typically passed down within a family maintaining generational and traditional hoodoo knowledge, although it can also be learned (Creel 1988: 52–57). One can be born with power and learn the skills to harness that power from established conjurers. Individuals can experience "a calling" to become a root doctor based upon visions and other clues to one's destiny (Chireau 2003: 23).

Hoodoo consists of a variety of magic spells with a range of positive to negative objectives from cultivating good luck to benefiting the individual or household, providing curative treatments for illnesses, divining the future, and offering protection. On the darker end of the spectrum there are curses and vengeance spells to do harm or to kill. Magic spells require specific objects for specific tasks to appeal to the correct supernatural entities and include but are not limited to: herbs, bodily fluids and other biological material, grave dirt (aka *goopher* dirt), photographs, written phrases or symbols, and more that are collected together (Chireau 2003: 48; Long 2001: 3–8). These are administered in a variety of ways in combination with recitation of magic utterances to bring about the desired outcome.

Too often, people outside of these cultural communities confuse or conflate hoodoo with voodoo, or Vodun, which is a religion most associated with Haiti and New Orleans where many Haitians relocated in the late 18th and early 19th centuries (Chireau 2003: 4). One high-profile individual was 19th-century Madame Laveau of New Orleans, who drew her knowledge from African, Native American, and European religions and who was frequently described as a voodoo queen, sorceresses, or conjurer. Madame Laveau is frequently the only model of reference because of her historical status among the general public; most people's understanding of African folk magic is based on what they think she stood for and practiced (Long 2001: 45–52). Santería (Cuba) and Candomblé (Brazil) are two more examples of African religions that have been highly exploited in the commercial and entertainment industry for their name recognition. There are many more that have been appropriated similarly but they are too numerous to mention here. This Element acknowledges the influences that many African religions and traditions have had on the public perception, often with misinformation, but they will not be covered in this Element because they are not relevant to the practices on the Hume Plantation.

Most African religions observe a hierarchy and formality with designated leaders that control rituals and services. To put it simply, hoodoo is differentiated from any single, specific religion and can be likened to the difference between a practicing psychic/healer (individual) using occult and mystical knowledge versus a religion's formally recognized leader (priest/reverend/pastor/imam/rabbi) performing a ritual that is structured by the religion that it directly represents.

Lest this leave the reader with the view that hoodoo conjurers were outliers viewed as less legitimate within the African community – African religions do not make distinctions between the power of the individual as illegitimate versus the power of a religion as the only legitimate expression. Comparatively, in a Christian society a prayer or exhortation is viewed as legitimate because it asks for or urges an intervention from a recognized supernatural entity, whether deity, saint, and so on, but spells or incantations are illegitimate because they are expressions of magic and an attempt to compel action from a supernatural entity. Invoking energies in this way is not hierarchically recognized as legitimate. In essence, it implies that the individual possesses more power than they have a right to wield and likely came into that power through nefarious means.

From an anthropological view, however, one person's prayer/exhortation is another person's spell/incantation; it depends upon how you wish to frame it linguistically and provide a label for which it may be accepted or denied. Another example would be the concept of inviting a spirit to possess the body, however transiently, by an individual who wishes the blessing of the spirit called upon – yet it is distinguished by some as less legitimate than inviting a "holy ghost" to reside within. Either can be viewed negatively or positively, depending upon one's perspective. Suffice it to say, Indigenous African peoples from the West and Central regions saw religion, magic, and spirituality as a combined whole of their Kongo cultural traditions (Chireau 2003: 38; Creel 1988: 19–21). Unfortunately, a pejorative use of the term "magic" is often applied to religions and practices that are not recognized or are feared by the dominant group in a society regardless of its intent. Its inherent Otherness robs it of legitimacy from the dominant society's view. For this reason, hoodoo and its other iterations have often been misunderstood and all expressions of it labeled "black magic."

It is important to remember that this Element will focus only on hoodoo practices on the Hume Plantation and the enslaved groups particular to the Lowcountry. For comparative purposes, some examples from other plantations will help to demonstrate the similarities where they are relevant.

In addition, it is not always possible to identify specific purposes for ritual/ magic deposits archaeologically. There may be patterns from which one can infer intent, based upon known use of materials and their treatment, but this is limited to a general understanding of "white magic" versus "black magic."

1.2 Cosmology and African Religions

African religions are not all the same, just as Native American belief systems are not all the same and vary from tribe to tribe and region to region. However, there are some basic concepts and frameworks that can be applied without compromising the uniqueness of each or reducing their spiritualities into a one-size-fits-all. It is important to understand this general framework in order to place hoodoo magic in its proper context.

A supreme deity is normally at the center of most African belief systems. Most often this deity is neither good nor evil and is frequently removed from the world of human beings and their daily triumphs and travails (Long 2001: 3–5). For this reason, there are lesser supernaturals to whom human beings can turn for assistance who may act to alter outcomes in one's life. The concept of intermediaries is particularly expressed in Fon and Yoruba belief systems (West and Central Africa) from where many of the enslaved in the Lowcountry originated. Successful persuasion of supernaturals and ancestral spirits to act resides in sufficient demonstrations of honor and reverence paid to them, and special knowledge of magic ingredients and use of one's power to attract and invoke them (Creel 1988; Long 2003: 3–5). Spirits and other supernatural entities may be benevolent or maleficent depending upon the nature of the request and their own personalities (Pinckney 2003: 65–79).

Within this general cosmological framework, items labeled as inanimate objects by other belief systems do not exist in an African perspective. Spirits and other supernatural entities can inhabit landscapes and their features such as rocks, plants, trees, and rivers, as well as forces of nature: storms, wind, lightning, and so on (Long 2003: 5). Animals and other nonhuman organisms may also harbor a supernatural entity.

1.3 Ritual and Magic Defined

The objects and deposits identified as ritualistic through the Hume Plantation Stave Street Project were designated so because they followed a specific and identifiable pattern of material use and placement. Ritual deposits are differentiated from cast-off activity in that they are purposeful rather than arbitrary and are placed in defined areas known for their magical or spiritual significance, rather than being left in unspecified general areas in and around the house that have no symbolic meaning. Objects found in trash pits or in general areas without the magical symbolism or context are interpreted as not part of the ritual pattern, and are simply cast-offs or misplaced items. Following Catherine Bell's (2009: 69–71) theories of ritual behavior, ritual deposits in the Hume Plantation slave quarter communicate more than passive requests; they are expressive acts of defiance and *strategy*. Interpreted in the context of enslavement, the actions of the enslaved can be seen both as formal and repetitive, interpreted as "passive," and as ritualized to invoke a specific outcome, which is interpreted as "active."

Bell discusses several modes of *instrumental* acts and clarifies that the combination of expressive and instrumental ritual can also constitute a definition of magic. Ritual communication to engage with ancestors, deities, and spirits to bring about a desired effect is taken together with unique acts designed to target individuals; they are considered together in this Element.

Archaeologically, a pattern emerged among the enslavement cabins that further reinforced and supported interpretations that certain objects constituted ritual activity. These patterns included but were not limited to: (1) deposits buried beneath the cabin floor but in line with the structural framework of the cabin wall(s); (2) deposits that were consistently placed equidistantly (approximately one meter or three feet apart) and contained similar and/or specific content materials; (3) deposits, varied in content, that tended to be concentrated around the hearth or chimney area on the south side of the cabin; (4) certain deposits concentrated in the corners of a structure's foundation that suggest a conscious directionality connected to spiritual or cosmological forces; (5) deposits placed in areas considered "liminal" spaces – such as entrances or exits, doorway thresholds (internal or external), and fence lines or gates.

Besides the initial twenty-one ritual deposits recognized in the initial excavations of the slave street that will be discussed in the following sections, there were special finds that were designated as anomalies due to the fact that there was no ready explanation for them yet they also appeared not to be randomly cast-off objects. The nature of these anomalous objects (for instance, their being made of an exotic material, something that would have been hard to acquire, make, or find, that had known associated symbolism), even though they were not placed in with other objects of similar symbolic or magical use, indicates that possibly the magical context has been lost or is unconfirmed in the excavation. Because there was no identifiable pattern due to their limited occurrences, they are noted separately from the twenty-one identified hoodoo deposits. However, noting them for future reference is important in the event that more is discovered. Ritual deposits appeared to suggest an ordering of the environment in such a way as to ensure that power was invoked for purpose; Bell would call this "instrumental" in combination with "expressive" communication with the supernatural world (Bell 2009: 79). These deposits were then compared to similar finds noted at other African American communities or enslavement sites for insight and possible ritual. Stand-alone ritual deposits are noted within the section categories where they are relevant.

1.4 Historical Use and Preservation of the Site

In historical archaeology, it is important to know the level of disturbance the site being studied may have undergone before it was excavated to know in what ways and how much, if at all, it has been compromised by human, animal, and environmental activities over time. Disturbances of the archaeological record and its evidence can affect the interpretation and understanding of the site. For this reason, a brief overview of the plantation era into the 20th century is included.

The Tom Yawkey Wildlife Center is a refuge that includes Cat, North, and South Islands and is located approximately 10 miles south of Georgetown, South Carolina. Today it serves as a conservation and sanctuary property for wildlife, birds (resident and special migratory), botanical species, estuary ecosystems, and ocean life off its coastal waters. Further, its status as a wildlife refuge helps to preserve historical/archaeological sites on its islands as well. The Hume Plantation on Cat Island is not to be confused with the Cat Island of Beaufort County, which is located between Charleston, South Carolina and Savannah, Georgia.

Cat Island is frequently the focus of several research projects from various institutions and scholars who study coastal flora and fauna. Until 2011, the only archaeological activity on Cat Island was an isolated surface survey conducted in 1993 as part of South Carolina's Heritage and Historic Preservation effort (Judge and Judge 1994). In 2011 the first archaeological exploration began with surface survey, test pits, and subsurface excavations conducted by the author and her students and volunteers in 2011, 2012, 2015, and 2017, culminating in a study season in 2018 and compilation of the data presented in this Element.

Cat, North, and South Islands have benefited from limited access since 1976 upon becoming a designated wildlife refuge. Prior to this designation, these lands were privately owned from the mid 18th century to contemporary times and saw minimal development beyond the plantations that were in operation during the historical period of the mid 18th to the mid 19th centuries. Limited access and growth are beneficial to historical archaeology studies. It is rare to find undisturbed and preserved archaeological evidence of ritual behaviors that has survived for over 150 years.

Unlike many historical sites that suffer from increasing modernization such as expanding agriculture and construction projects to keep up with population growth, Cat and South Islands have had limited population and low numbers have been consistent over time. North Island is perhaps least populated, is more isolated, and functions as a barrier island across the Winyah Bay. North Island is first to engage with destructive weather fronts coming in from the northeastern Atlantic and offers some protection to Cat and South Islands. Besides being a weather barrier, North Island has a topography that is also resistant to habitation. Its coastal edges are made up of wide sandy dunes punctuated throughout with wet marshy swales and further inland are live oak, cedar, and palmetto trees.[1]

Because of its less hospitable environment and weather conditions, North Island is not suitable for general habitation. It is better suited to other purposes, such as a lighthouse, one of which was constructed there in 1799 and referred to as the Georgetown Lighthouse (Zepke 1998). It was rebuilt twice during the 19th century: once because of damage from brutal storms that struck the barrier hardest and a second time for repair due to damage incurred during a Civil War–era military engagement. The lighthouse functioned as a lookout tower for the Confederate army until its capture by the Union army in 1862 (Zepke 1998).

To accommodate the rice plantations, canals were dredged on Cat and South Islands mainly for irrigation and drainage. The Belle Isle Rice Mill, also known as (aka) Black Out Plantation, was created to process the rice generated by the plantations (Lachicotte 1993: 161–166). In addition, there were two Confederate forts built one year after South Carolina seceded from the Union in 1860. In 1861 one fort was placed on Cat Island and the other on South Island. These were strategically located to oversee and provide fortification over Winyah Bay, but they were short-lived and abandoned the following year because the troops were sorely needed elsewhere (Giauque et al. 2010: 111).

Naval stores were harvested mainly for British interests in the 18th century, but this ended with the Revolutionary War. The islands have a healthy forest of long-leaf pine that provided a source for tar and resin rendering and turpentine,

---

[1] National Estuarine Research (NERR), https://northinlet.sc.edu.

which was necessary once more in the 19th century for shipbuilding, but this was again a short-term endeavor.

Throughout this period, Cat and South Islands were home to descendant communities. While a few stayed on after emancipation in 1865, others left the islands to reside in nearby Georgetown or farther south along what is now Interstate 17, the highway corridor to Charleston (today they are known as the Gullah Community), or they ventured inland to other unincorporated, largely African American communities.

The Hume Plantation, the Daisy Bank Plantation, the Chat/Cat Island Plantation (Smith family), White Marsh aka the Maxwell Plantation (Maxwell family), the Fairfield Plantation, and Belle Isle aka Black Out Plantation (Lowndes family) thrived on Cat and South Islands from the antebellum through the Civil War era as successful rice plantations (Lachicotte 1993; Land 1969; Rogers 2002).

Cat Island plantations' former rice fields slowly fell into disuse as the grounds were no longer cultivated. In the aftermath of the Civil War, large tracts of plantation grounds including the rice fields were slowly reclaimed by the environment. The rice industry could not be maintained without sufficient funds. Former rice plantations could not compete with rice industry competitors in other states and the economy collapsed. Competitors in Arkansas, Texas, Louisiana, and California had the advantage of new technology and machinery not available in the aftermath of the Civil War South (Sea Grant Consortium 2014).

Descendant African American populations that stayed on Cat Island began an unincorporated town in the 1920s known as the Maxwell Community (Giauque et al. 2010). Traffic was limited and there was no need for large construction projects. Much of the bull pine found around the Hume Plantation slave street today is considered relatively new growth – having sprung up in the last sixty to eighty years. Oak and hickory trees, dwarf spike rush, marsh grass, cattails, widgeon grass, and kudzu provide thick ground cover. Some root disturbances of shrubbery and ground cover were ameliorated when the Yawkey Wildlife Center periodically practiced forest management and burned or cut shrubbery and accumulated duff to prevent risk of insect or vegetation disease. This was particularly true of the Hume Plantation slave street, which was preserved by keeping the underbrush and tree growth controlled on the east side where the majority of excavations were done.

Small personal garden plots were common among descendants much the same as they were for their ancestors. Some former slaves continued to inhabit the cabins, but their numbers diminished as lumber and other reusable resources from the cabins were repurposed elsewhere. As a result, ground disturbance from plow and/or other machinery was minimal to nonexistent in many places.

The St. James African Methodist Episcopal (AME) church was constructed in 1928 to serve the small community until 1979 (Giauque et al. 2010). A small fishing village was born on the South Island shoreline in the late 19th century, but did not survive coastal storms and erosion. The population continued to diminish between 1865 and 1976, which promoted near-pristine conditions for preserving the ruins of former plantation grounds even though many of the above-ground structures were deconstructed and materials were repurposed elsewhere. What was left fell into ruin or succumbed to coastal storms.

1.5 Environmental Factors

We can say that there was limited human disturbance of the pre- and historical eras, and that helped preserve archaeological sites and artifacts on the Hume Plantation. However, it is worth noting that there were some environmental conditions that impacted the types of artifact that survived in the archaeological record. The Lowcountry can suffer from seasonal storms, hurricanes, and flooding. Undergrowth is generally heavy in areas where controlled burning and other maintenance procedures are not applied. Topsoil and subsurface excavation reflect sporadic disruption at depths of 5 to 10 centimeters (approximately 4 inches) when topsoil has been moved due to hurricane and storm surge. This is generally identified within Level 1 – considered within a 20th-century time frame – and is of limited scope.

On the three islands, the forest and heavy undergrowth that are present limit movement of soils. It is important to remember that the levels assigned to the stratigraphy are an artificial designation and there is overlap between Level 1 and Level 2, for instance. For clarity, objects found in the mid to lower range of Level 1 or the upper range of Level 2 may be within the same time frame. Thus, some flexibility should be applied to interpretive analysis when within a few centimeters or inches above or below the mid range.

There were no agricultural plow zones and no construction damage in the Hume Plantation slave street area, as these spaces were intermittently inhabited as residences in the post–Civil War era but slowly abandoned over the intervening years between 1865 and 1900. Flooding action was considered a possibility for topsoil disturbances where applicable, such that artifacts nearer the surface (20th-century level) may have been displaced. Ocean and/or canal water that overflowed inland could have possibly introduced artifacts from other contexts and deposited them in unrelated, noncontextual places. These factors were taken into consideration in the process of interpreting and understanding the associations within assemblages of Level 1 finds.

Bioturbation and artifact displacement due to root growth and animal tunneling was also considered for all excavated levels. Artifacts found embedded near root systems were noted, along with any observable small rodent activity. Despite this, much of the artifact deposits designated as evidence of ritual were found to be in patterned, purposeful placements that counter arguments of random, coincidental, or unrelated finds and the majority were found along the somewhat protected structural remnants of the foundations of the slave cabins, sheds, and fence lines. Deposits of a unique nature found in backyards, unassociated with any man-made structure, were also noted. In those cases, root growth disturbance was noted where it could be seen. Most of these stand-alone deposits were excavated in Levels 2, 3, or 4 – which placed them deeper than surface and Level 1 disturbances would have reached. Much of the new tree growth root systems and animal tunneling was recent, meaning that it was not significant enough to disturb object placements in lower levels.

The soil matrix in this area is a combination of silty/clay loam. The topsoil along the Hume Plantation slave street proved to be rich and fertile, going down to a depth of approximately 20–30 centimeters (8–12 inches) in most areas and in some places 40 centimeters (approximately 16 inches), good for backyard gardens that most of the enslaved utilized around their cabins. Areas near the canals and irrigation ditches do not tend to drain well and shovel tests, depending upon proximity to them, could produce slow seepage or moist soils.

The acidity/alkalinity of the soils on the slave street was tested and results showed a pH of 3–4 on a scale of 0–14, where 7 is considered neutral. Readings below 7 are acidic (and increasingly so as it nears 1); soils at 7pH or above are more alkaline, which is more conducive to preservation. The Hume Plantation slave street soils would be considered very acidic. High pH levels (acidity) accelerate the decomposition process of bone and organic material. There are a few exceptions that would survive for an extended length of time (i.e., teeth, burned carbon, hickory nut shells, marine shells). Thus, certain artifact types could be over- or underrepresented, leading to a skewed understanding of certain practices, and this, too, was taken into consideration during interpretation.

The topography along the Lowcountry of Georgetown County is mainly flat with a high percentage of new growth forests (120 years or less) of bull pine. There are a few surviving "old growth" mature hardwood trees of the oak variety, growing mainly in the area where the plantation Main House had been. Live oaks were noted on the Hume Plantation from early 20th-century photographs with some still standing today that are clearly over 150 years old; these were present in the antebellum through the Civil War and post–Civil War eras and serve as landmarks to aid in reconstructing the location of the slave street structures and proximity to the Main House when the surface survey was done.

1.6 The Yawkey Wildlife Center Legacy 1911–1977

Tom Yawkey originally inherited South Island in 1919 from his uncle and adoptive father, William Yawkey. William owned South Island from 1911 until he died on March 5, 1919 in the influenza pandemic that claimed the lives of approximately 675,000 people in the United States over a two-year period, according to the National Archives. Over the course of several years after coming into his inheritance of South Island, Tom Yawkey also acquired more oceanfront property and Cat and North Islands for 31 square miles of wetlands and forests (Giauque et al. 2010). These were bordered on the south by the Santee River. Cat Island has a unique fresh to saltwater estuary and thus unique aquatic life, reptiles, and migratory birds.

The three islands were used throughout the early to mid 20th century by the Yawkeys as a private, limited access getaway for elites like themselves; they hosted a members-only hunting club. Upper-social-class personalities were invited to visit Cat Island to stay in a lodge and experience the wilderness, engage in hunting and fishing activities, and enjoy seclusion away from the hubbub of city life and the society pages. Willliam and Tom Yawkey's social circle included baseball players and politicians of the late 19th and early 20th centuries such as President Grover Cleveland and Ty Cobb of the Boston Red Sox. The Yawkey family was known as "baseball royalty," with William owning the Detroit Tigers from 1903 to 1919 (until his death) and then Tom Yawkey as owner of the Boston Red Sox from 1933 to 1976 (Giauque et al. 2010).

The Yawkey Wildlife Center was set up in 1976–1977 when the owner, Tom Yawkey, willed the islands to the state of South Carolina Wildlife and Marine Resources Department. The Center was to be maintained by the South Carolina Department of Natural Resources (SCDNR), and the Yawkey Foundation (a nonprofit, charitable organization) was to oversee its funding.

The Yawkey Wildlife Center has appointed personnel for limited times during the weekdays since the 1970s to provide a ferry service. A floating hydraulic swing bridge was installed in 2015 to make access easier; it eliminated the need for the ferry except under special circumstances. The swing bridge has limited operation times, as did the ferry, and was installed because it became necessary to move heavier machinery and the vehicles of the island residents, mainly employees of the SCDNR, and to transport supplies such as fuel and other essentials.

Today, the Center's islands continue to enforce limited access and most who visit must do so by prearranged day tours and guided field trips. The Estherville-Minim Creek Canal carved out what became Cat Island by artificially separating it from the mainland of Georgetown County. The Estherville-Minim Creek

Canal was constructed at the end of the 19th century (Giauque et al. 2010; see also the SCDNR website[2]). The Intracoastal Waterway was added in the early to mid 20th century and together these canals act as a barrier restricting land passage onto the Center's islands. For over a century, access has been possible only by a brief manned-ferry-boat ride.

2 Beginnings of Slave Trade in Winyah Bay: Native Americans enslaved by Spanish and British Colonizers, 16th–18th Centuries

It is important to establish a historical development of the plantation system in the South Carolina Lowcountry and Native Americans' role within that early system for two reasons: (1) context in any archaeological endeavor is a core concern for interpretation and understanding and (2) the interaction historically between Native Americans, Europeans, and Africans is important to understanding the ritual, symbolic, and cultural practices that were born out of that interaction and that contribute to the theme of this Element.

The Spanish were the first Europeans to arrive in the Carolinas' Winyah Bay area by the early 16th century. The area would become known as South Carolina after the land base was formally separated into northern and southern halves in 1712. The Lords Proprietors appointed a governor and a deputy governor to administer the vast swatch of land by 1691 and within twenty-two years they became separate colonies (Walbert 2008). The Spanish were looking for sites to establish colonies and eager to acquire Native Americans for the slave trade. Their first colonizing attempt was known as San Miguel de Guadalupe and was in what is now Georgetown County. The settlement was officially christened in September 1526 (Peck 2001). However, the colony was short-lived – by some accounts lasting less than two months – due to Native hostilities in retaliation for Spanish slaving activities, disease, and settlers' inability to secure sufficient foodstuffs. It was in the fall season – too late to attempt agriculture, and inadequate familiarity with the environment meant failure in hunting and gathering attempts. The Spanish had been awaiting a ship filled with supplies to relieve them, but it had shipwrecked, never to arrive.[3] The remaining Spanish colonists abandoned San Miguel de Guadalupe and relocated farther south into Georgia where the terrain was less unforgiving.

Natives in the Winyah Bay and immediate coastal area were primarily represented by small groups such as the Westo, the Chicora, the Sewees, the Santees,

---

[2] South Carolina Department of Natural Resources (SCDNR), www.dnr.sc.gov/.
[3] Gilder Lehrman Institute of American History (GLIAH), www.gilderlehrman.org/ap-us-history/period-1.

the Sampits, the Winyaws, the Peedees, the Yamassee, and the Waccamaws, to name but a few (Gallay 2002; Rogers 2002; Swanton 1946). Over time, smaller groups suffered the most from slaving activities and the constant threat of abductions. Intertribal warfare fed slaving activities when tribes began selling their enemy captives to European slavers. Smaller, vulnerable tribes adopted a survival strategy of banding together with larger tribes; their separate identities evolved as they became subsumed. Many original coastal tribal groups had figuratively "vanished" by 1755 and were no longer identifiable as separate entities. Only the larger groups maintained their ancestral identity (Lauber 2002; Rogers 2002).

There is speculation and a persistent popular myth that European diseases were responsible for the devastating population losses of the coastal South Carolina Natives. While diseases certainly contributed, there is no doubt, given the scale of the Native slave trade in the late 17th to the early 18th centuries, however, that enslavement itself was the primary catalyst for Native population dispersal in addition to large-scale exposure to diseases, dissemination, and loss (Gallay 2002; Lauber 2002; Rogers 2002).

By 1542, Spain had passed its "New Laws" that limited slaving from among Native American tribes along southeastern North America. This caveat was implemented because Queen Isabella of Spain felt conflicted about enslaving people who were technically her subjects since the entire coastal area had been claimed as Spanish territory. Spanish colonists had already begun enforcing Catholicism and prohibiting Native spiritual beliefs among subjected Indians. Thus, Spain had created for itself an even larger ethical and moral conundrum (Gallay 2002).

Despite that, slaving was far too important economically for Spain to abolish it completely; likewise for other European countries that participated in the slave trade. A 1542 Spanish law allowed slavers to capture Native Americans whom they deemed cannibals, though identifying which Natives fit into that category and enforcing the criteria appear to have been routinely circumvented.[4] Many slave traders continued business as usual, unabated. A major loophole allowed slave traders to continue acquiring Native slaves legally, as long as they were purchased from other Europeans or other Natives, such as the Westo, who sold enemy captives as a common practice (Gallay 2002).

Meanwhile, the British challenged Spain for dominance in the Southeast. By 1587 the Spanish had given up on Carolina and focused their efforts on Florida and Georgia instead. The British were much more successful in colonizing what eventually became designated as South Carolina, investing resources and bringing in settlers regularly. By 1663, King Charles II had approved eight

---

[4] GLIAH – see n. 3.

Lord's Proprietors from among the English nobility who, in the interest of rewarding their loyalty to him through difficult times and for the sake of British colonizing in North America, were awarded land grants in Carolina to encourage development and contribute to the British economic system. This provided lucrative incentives for British settlers to come to Carolina. In 1670, the British colony of Charleston was established (North Carolina Department of Natural and Cultural Resources [NC-DNCR] 2016).

Unlike British commoners and other European immigrants who arrived from Germany, Ireland, Scandinavia, Italy, Poland, and Russia to the northeastern colonies, those flooding into South Carolina arrived with a much different agenda and economic background. The earliest arrivals to South Carolina were mainly British aristocrats with strong ties to Britain that they wished to maintain and enhance. Their primary goal was to expand their businesses into the New World and to build wealth, not to start anew or escape the British system. Some of these aristocrats already had plantations in the West Indies, in Jamaica and Barbados, of sugar cane, tobacco, coffee, and cotton. Enslaved Africans were a long-established part of this economic system. These British elites did not bond as a community with the commoner class of newcomers or with their agenda of starting a new life in the New World. Instead, British aristocrats with land grants connected to other British elites like themselves, primarily for business ventures and social interaction, and established a class-based society with its own traditions early on.

According to Gallay (2002: 299), between 1670 and 1715 Carolina exported more [Indian] slaves than it imported before 1715. There may not have been a single year in the colony before 1715, except for 1714, when the number of slaves imported exceeded the number of Indians exported. Charles Town, as Peter H. Wood incisively shows, was an Ellis Island for Africans arriving in the New World; but it also marked the point of deportation for thousands of Native Americans. This does not account for the unknown numbers of Native Americans who were kept within the colonies, mainly sold to British plantation owners in North and South Carolina and Virginia, who began establishing plantations by the late 17th century (National Park Service [NPS] 2017).

Enslaved Native Americans sold within the southern colonies proved problematic for their European owners. After enslavement, exposure to Old World diseases sickened and proved fatal to a significant number of them. In addition, coastal tribes knew nothing of the cultivation and harvesting strategies necessary for plantations' mass production cash crops. This, too, added to mortality rates and escapees being a constant concern. Unlike indentured Europeans and enslaved Africans, escaped Natives could survive in the unforgiving environment with which they were familiar. Frequently retreating into the forests, backwaters, and swamps, or deeper into the uplands and away from European settlements altogether, enslaved Native runaways were almost impossible to reclaim. Recapture efforts more often than not proved unsuccessful and costly. For all these reasons, British plantation owners shifted their approach and sought enslaved Africans, with whom they had a history and familiarity, even though enslaved Africans commanded a higher price on the slave market. As far as enslaved Natives were concerned, it was more fruitful to ship them overseas to places that would essentially isolate them in unfamiliar environments, urban centers, and among foreign populations.

Indigo was the main crop for the South Carolina Lowcountry during the late 17th and into the early 18th centuries. Cotton was a growing economic interest in British colonies, including South Carolina, as a mass production commercial crop and also as a family farm venture. Cotton was uniformly exported back to England in vast amounts during the Industrial Revolution to supply the burgeoning textile industry at that time (Butler 2019). A high demand for indigo dye coincided with the growing cotton market and lasted well into the late 18th century.

It is difficult to account for the number of enslaved Native Americans on fledgling plantations on Cat, South, and North Islands during the 17th and 18th centuries among the enslaved Africans. Part of the problem stems from the practice at the time of recording their number as "colored" on plantation property records; a cursory examination of historical archives confirms this as a common and widespread practice. At times the only distinguishing information about ethnic identity comes from descendants themselves, through family stories and experiences during the American Depression of 1929–1941 (McEwan 2000; Minges 2004) told to the WPA as part of President Roosevelt's New Deal economic stimulus of the FWP from 1935 to 1939. These interviews were conducted during the lifetimes of freed slaves and their children who could still recall the experiences in first-person accounts.

Anyone who was not Caucasian was by default a person of color and labeled "colored." Enslaved Africans were referred to as "Negro" on plantation ledgers – and later the term "mulatto" was inconsistently used to identify those of mixed heritage (mainly African and Caucasian). Mixed African/Native American and Native/Caucasian continued to be classified as "Negro" or "colored."[5] Native American enrollment records tend to distinguish between those counted as Native and those counted as "freedmen" (National Archives 1790–1870). Furthermore, specific African tribal identities were not documented on purchasing receipts or

---

[5] National Archives Records Administration (NARA), Slave Schedule, Microfilm series M653, Roll 1235, www.archives.gov/research/census/microfilm-catalog/1790-1890/part-04#south-carolina (accessed September 19, 2024).

ownership titles. More important to the plantation owner was gender, age (childbearing or not), and whether the enslaved had farming knowledge or, more specifically, knew how to grow and cultivate rice. Sometimes ledgers reflect an enslaved person's special skills, like blacksmithing (Cuddy and Leone 2008).

European bureaucrats tried to maintain this manner of accounting into the late 19th and 20th centuries and were confronted with resistance from some Natives who refused to be described as "colored." Mixed heritage individuals whose last known African ancestor was a grandparent or even further removed were still legally classified as "Negro" under the "one-drop rule." The one-drop rule was legally passed in Southern states in the early 20th century but had been an informal cultural practice for generations. It quickly spread as a legal standard for labeling individuals. The one-drop rule mandated that anyone with even one African ancestor, no matter how distant in one's background, was forever identified as "black" or "Negro" (Lerch 2004; Sharfstein 2007).

Equally rarely do we find records that list enslaved Native Americans' tribal relationships because this was not considered important or necessary information. The official United States census began in 1790 in South Carolina after the colony had ratified the United States Constitution. They continued use of the term "colored" for nearly another century and a half.[6]

It is impossible to provide a definitive number of enslaved Natives on Cat, South, or North Island plantations given the obstacles inherent in the style of recordkeeping at the time. We can, however, consider the extensive history of Spanish and British slave trading in the area – roughly 200 years of victimizing Indigenous peoples by the mid 18th century – and conclude that there is a high probability that enslaved Indigenous people were indeed present at the earliest stages of European colonizing efforts around the Winyah Bay. Material evidence from archaeological excavations also suggests that there were likely mixed heritage families on Cat Island in the 18th century and/or knowledge of both Indigenous and African culture among them by the time the Hume Plantation was a producing rice plantation in the early 19th century. In addition, there can be little doubt that interactions between Native "friendlies" and enslaved Africans were ongoing before and after the Hume family had acquired the land on Cat Island.

The number of enslaved Natives diminished significantly throughout the 17th to the early 18th centuries; by 1750, the overwhelming majority of enslaved people in the South Carolina Lowcountry were African. Enslaved Natives could not fulfill the labor needs and expectations of the plantation owners, most of

---

[6] NARA – see n. 5.

whom had switched from indigo to rice production. As the demand for indigo lessened, it became a secondary crop one could grow along the riverbanks.

Indigo required only well-drained but fertile soil and sunlight most of the day. Constant weeding was the most labor-intensive activity necessary to prevent vulnerable indigo plants from being choked off by competitive wild plants. Indigo planting and growing seasons were also very compatible with the rice since rice crops required the marshier/wetter, undrained soil and a longer growing season (about four months). The two crops could share an overlap in space and resources and make most efficient use of the labor on a plantation during this crossover period. Plantation owners could still reap income while they secured the slave labor and expertise needed to clear the land and dig trenches and marshes to accommodate the shift of commercial crops from indigo to rice (SCDNR 2022).

Indigo demand effectively ended with the Revolutionary War. Rice had completely taken over as the main cash crop by then and continued to be the number one economic interest until the second half of the 19th century. It was necessary to turn wetlands and swamps into rice paddies and irrigation canals. The challenge of establishing a successful rice plantation was always the monumental labor it took to reshape the landscape and find sufficient expertise among the enslaved who knew rice. The majority of the plantation owners did not have that knowledge. Special canal locks became necessary to control the fresh-to-saltwater estuaries throughout the coastal region. The innovation of the special lock system proved vital to the rice plantation enterprise.

Early British aristocratic arrivals in South Carolina initially brought small numbers of their enslaved Africans. In early colonization efforts, most of the enslaved were left working on established plantations in the West Indies. The slave trade flourished, and African slaves were imported in ever-increasing numbers once it became obvious that plantation owners needed slaves that were more familiar with the marshy and coastal environments. By the early 18th century, the African population outnumbered the Europeans. By the mid 18th century, enslaved Africans from the West (Gold Coast) were sought because rice farming was a part of their culture in their homeland. Gold Coast slaves commanded the highest prices on the slave market in Charleston because they knew rice and had the necessary skills to make it a profitable crop in the Lowcountry (Giauque et al. 2010).

According to Georgetown County archival records, in 1711 a French Huguenot named Bartholomew Gaillard was the first to own property in the area that would later become South Island (Giauque et al. 2010). Gaillard initially focused his efforts on raising cattle. A number of landowners utilized their enslaved Africans (Congolese) as "cowboys" to oversee the livestock until more profitable ventures were discovered that could replace it.

There is also a Bartholomew Gaillard listed as the Superintendent in the Indian Department of British North America (the equivalent of the US Bureau of Indian Affairs) in Berkeley County, which borders Georgetown County, in 1716. Bartholomew Gaillard ran an Indian trading post outside historic Jamestown, South Carolina along the Santee River, which also lies within Berkeley County (Cross 1985; Gourdin 2023). Trade thrived with "friendly" Natives who were non-hostile to British interests, and who sometimes served as British allies, such as the Waccamaw who sided with the British against the Tuscarora Indians. Native furs, pottery, and other resources were commonly exchanged for European cookware and coveted weaponry (Lerch 2004). The enslaved Africans also traded with Natives; family garden-plot produce and handmade items were exchanged for wild meat and botanical knowledge. Native influence can be seen in two ritual deposits that repurposed a projectile point and a biface on Hume Plantation grounds.

Historic Jamestown is approximately 22 miles northwest of McClellanville and 30 miles west of Georgetown and South Island. Bartholomew Gaillard of South Island is listed in property records (1706) as residing in Berkeley County. He was a landholder near Charleston as well (Langley 1984). As other settlers moved into the Georgetown area, raising cattle was their main interest until other cash crops became more viable, providing more return on investment. At this time, most enslaved peoples were composed of Native peoples, supplemented by enslaved Africans. Within a span of fifty years, that ratio would be reversed and eventually enslaved African numbers would completely replace Native enslaved populations.

Gaillard was eventually joined by other early British settlers around Winyah Bay. These included George Ford Sr., who also acquired property on South Island and established the Ford Plantation in 1760. The Ford family was to own property there for over a century, expanding into Cat Island and lasting as a Ford estate throughout the Civil War period (Giauque et al. 2010). Eventually, the Ford and the Hume families became related by marriage, and a section of Ford property on Cat Island became Hume family property.

According to Georgetown County land records, the Hume Plantation was in existence by 1825 or 1827; the exact date of its establishment is unclear as there is reference to both dates and a hand-drawn plat map created in 1827 indicates a number of slave cabins and other structures already in place (see Figure 3). It is speculated that the development of the plantation grounds and acquisition of enslaved people was a process over time and carried over from previous property owners and earlier indigo cultivation. It may be that the land was

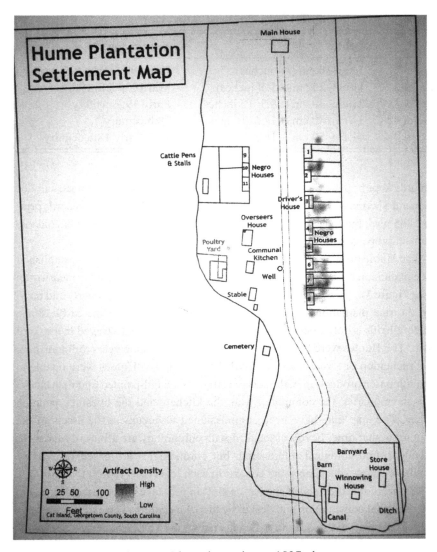

Figure 3 Hume Plantation redrawn 1827 plat map.

Source: Illustration by the author.

technically owned by the Humes by 1825, but that the plantation as a Hume family endeavor was not fully realized until 1827.

Much of the history prior to the Civil War of property ownership on Cat, South, and North Islands and Georgetown County in general is pieced together from fragments of surviving Georgetown County records in combination with other historical documents such as personal diaries, letters, census records from the first official South Carolina census in 1790, and, later, copies of original county

Table 1 Levels and chronology

	Depth	Year range
Level 1	1 cm–10 cm (~4 inches)	Late 19th–early 20th century
Level 2	11 cm–20 cm (~5–8 inches)	Mid 19th–late 19th century
Level 3	21 cm–30 cm (~8.5–12 inches)	Early 19th century
Level 4	31 cm–40 cm (~12.5–16 inches)	18th century
Level 4+	41 cm–50 cm (~16.5–20 inches)	17th–early 18th century

records kept by landowners themselves. Georgetown County was a casualty of General Sherman's scorched earth policy in that most of its original records prior to 1865 were burned (Langley 1984; Rogers 2002). Thus, there are unavoidable gaps in property ownership and timelines.

The Hume property appears to have been fully functioning as an established rice plantation by 1827, implying that it had evolved from an earlier incarnation (see Figure 3). It is estimated that the Humes came to own the property and build up the rice plantation sometime around the late 1790s into the early 1800s, although this is only a best guess as property records were destroyed in the Civil War. The Humes were the owners of record for thirty-nine years, relinquishing the plantation one year after the Civil War ended. The Humes were unable to maintain rice production without slave labor. The hand-painted plat map shows the slave quarter, the communal well, the kitchen, and the livestock penning areas. The map may have been commissioned to document the assets of the Humes at that time. Levels associated with chronology are arbitrarily fixed for standard archaeological referencing, but chronologies are based on relative dating methods of artifacts and context in each level (see Table 1).

Archaeological evidence suggests a shift in the slave street from informal to more formal construction and design by the 19th century. The earlier dwellings appear simpler and smaller than is reflected on the 1827 plat map.

There are rumors that when the Spanish colonists abandoned San Miguel de Guadalupe, a few stayed around South and Cat Islands (which were not yet islands but part of the mainland in Georgetown County). However, at the time of this writing, the author is unaware of any archaeological evidence that supports a Spanish presence on the islands.

2.1 Native American Seasonal Use of Cat Island

There is evidence of prehistoric Native campsites on Cat Island located in what was later to become the Hume Plantation slave quarter. Native pottery, charcoal and carbon residue from firepits, and lithic debitage in those levels and shovel tests indicate a presence of frequent use, though not a sedentary village occupation.

Early subsurface excavation on Cat Island indicates that prehistoric Natives were utilizing the area regularly. There was no evidence of long-term habitation but there was evidence of transitory (hunting) campsites (Swanton 1946). Evidence of transitory campsites included limited lithics debitage and ceramic pieces that had been fire-hardened with local sand temper for quick results and thus did not reflect a great deal of time and effort having been taken in their production. Quickly produced ceramics are those that are typically exposed to shorter firing times and at lower or inconsistent temperatures, often in a hearth or open fire pit. The result is ceramic material that has not had enough time and high heat exposure to completely bond the materials in comparison to those that are kiln fired. The ceramic is characterized by a hardened but coarse texture and has a shorter life-use.

Deptford ceramics (800 BCE–700 CE) from the Middle Woodland period in South Carolina is present at the lowest levels beneath the Hume Plantation slave street centuries later (see Table 2). Corded/fabric-stamped Deptford and Yadkin ceramics (1000 BCE–200 CE) tempered with crushed micacious bits or quartz (Trinkley 1990) have been found. Some prehistoric pottery and lithic pieces were repurposed in ritual deposits on the slave street.

Table 2 Prehistoric Native artifacts – lithics, pottery, charcoal

Lithic evidence	
Material/description	**Depth**
Rose quartz (lithic core)	Level 3
Worked stone (flint; debitage)	Levels 3, 4
Rhyolite debitage/flakes	Levels 4, 5, 6
Worked stone (scraper)	Shovel test (65 cm deep)
White quartz debitage/flakes	Shovel test (65 cm deep)
Native pottery	
Deptford (800 BCE–700 CE)	Levels 3, 4
Pee Dee corded/fabric impressed (1150–1400 CE)	Levels 3, 4
Micaceous/incised, zigzag, red/black	Levels 3, 4, 5
Plain ceramics: beige, red, black, thin	Levels 3, 4, 5
Yadkin (1000 BCE–200 CE)	Levels 4, 5
Pink w/shell temper, thin	Levels 7, 8
Charcoal/carbon – fire pit	
Charcoal pieces from a fire pit	Levels 3, 4, 5

Based on ceramic and temporary encampment evidence, Native groups had been utilizing the coastal resources of Cat and South Islands regularly from 1200 BCE up to the early 16th century with the arrival of the Spanish. They took advantage of natural resources when available, harvesting wild plants and hunting in seasonal rounds that followed an established yearly route from the uplands to the lowlands and back.

Small groups stayed for limited periods of time along the Lowcountry coast. It is likely that they chose not to establish long-term communities in close proximity to the coast due to environmental conditions: hurricane/storm season, tornadoes, high temperature and humidity, and concentrations of insects, snakes, and other troublesome conditions that plagued the region during the summer months (Gallay 2002). This prompted most Natives to travel inland for part of the year.

Alternatively, most coastal resource harvesting, that is, hunting, fishing, digging shellfish, and plant-gathering activities along the Lowcountry coastline, was done in the fall through the winter months. Ironically, this is the same season in which the 16th-century Spanish colonists of San Miguel de Guadalupe were struggling to survive due to ignorance of the abundance around them, and how and where to reap those resources. Deer hunting season is best in the late fall, before the deer go into rut in late October and early November; marine/shellfish harvesting reaches its most productive period from the late fall to early spring; and wild fruits such as apples, berries, and asparagus common to the area and many medicinal and cooking herbs such as sage, mint, basil, savory, and parsley are ready in the late autumn, winter, and/or early spring months (McEwan 2000; Mitchell 1999).

2.2 Native American Symbolism and Medicinal Knowledge

What we know of pre–European contact Native American ritual practices in the southeastern United States is limited and mainly learned through later accounts by missionaries (Gallay 2002; McEwan 2000). There are few accounts detailing the cosmology and ritual practices of South Carolina Natives in the Colonial period. Most early European–Native interactions were fueled by enslavement practices or attempts at conversion to Christianity rather than ethnographic preservation of traditional knowledge (Gallay 2002:105, 120–122, 237–238).

The Southeastern and Lowcountry tribes underwent significant changes in their culture and ideologies over the 200+ years of European contact. It cannot be overstated that loss of tribal knowledge and traditions, and loss of population due to disease, war, and absorption into other tribal entities, redefined identity such that it would be completely different within two generations of pre– to post–European contact. Today, Native efforts to recapture traditional knowledge are ongoing, but, unfortunately, much of it has been influenced by contemporary sources rather than being preserved ancestral knowledge, due to the circumstances of population loss (Lerch 2004; Rogers 2002).

What we know of Southeastern Native culture in mixed ethnic ritual display is largely linked to medicinal/curative and nutritional knowledge of plants in the Lowcountry. Herbal expertise was shared with enslaved African peoples who combined that knowledge with their own as they sought to find plants that offered the same benefits as those known from their African homelands (Mitchell 1999; Russell 1997; Savit 1978).

The Native perspectives on the environment, the seasons, the four sacred cardinal directions from which power over different aspects of life radiated, the ancestors, and the symbols of power share similarities in a general sense with the perspectives of many other Native Americans in the United States. Yet, specific details and practices between tribes differ.

In comparing the archaeological record of the Hume Plantation slave street to other archaeological contexts in the South, it is important to remember that the fundamental purposes for communicating with the spirit world were about curatives, protection, and divination. Black magic was also practiced to bring about harm or death, but at the Hume Plantation there is only one magic deposit that suggests ill intent; the second is indeterminate.

Ritual deposits found on the Hume Plantation suggest a synthesis of Native spirituality that overlapped and shared commonality with African concepts about ancestors, protection, and curatives. Herbal knowledge about curatives was undoubtedly the main point of shared knowledge between the African and the Native communities (Mitchell 1999). We can infer that there was perceived to be certain symbolism and cosmological value in specific Native-made objects that were included in ritual or magical deposits by the enslaved only through their association with other items in the magical deposits. Most of the decorative elements of the prehistoric ceramics are cord impressed lines or basic stamped geometric shapes made when the clay was wet. Pictorial imagery of animals and other objects was not part of the ceramic style, thus we cannot assign specific symbolic meaning incorporated from Native ideologies associated with animals, plants, and so on. Therefore, the symbolism may be more aligned with the Native American and/or prehistoric origins themselves, as perhaps an acknowledgment of ancestors and the past, or the natural earthern materials from which items were made, or possibly the color – although, because of the clay, that was largely a ubiquitous red-brown. That said, pieces of European and imported ceramics with bold painted colors were favored for specific color in African cosmological symbolism. Projectile points (also known as arrowheads) were found in magical deposits in two places on the slave street. The repurposing of these may be connected to the symbolism of items as weapons, as sharp edges, or as tools of resistance or protection. In any event, the repurposing of Native American-made objects where they were found in the enslaved's ritual and magical deposits demonstrates that the Native American component was considered sufficiently valid in some symbolic way to be incorporated into the deposits.

3 Hoodoo Rituals: Hiding in Plain Sight

Hoodoo technically arrived with enslaved Africans in the transatlantic slave trade to the South Carolina Lowcountry and all along the southeastern coast of North America in the 17th and 18th centuries. Hoodoo was particular to African groups in the Lowcountry who later came to be called Gullah or Gullah/Geechee in communities along the coastal regions of North and South Carolina, Georgia, and Florida, and who were brought in from Western Africa – Ghana, Sierra Leone, and Guinea – also known as the "Gold Coast" region (Creel 1988). The Gold Coast was home to the Yoruba, the Dahomey, the Ewe, and the Bakongo peoples. Other groups were brought in from Central Africa (Kongo). Most had already felt the influence of Christianity from the Portuguese who colonized those regions on the African continent from the 15th century onward (Creel 1988). The Portuguese had introduced Catholicism (Creel 1988; Singleton 1999). Catholic concepts were further reinforced in the early 20th century from 1908 to 1960. Belgium occupied Congo between 1885 and 1908, under the private ownership of King Leopold, when it was known as the Congo Free State (Momodu 2023).

One hoodoo practice brought to the Lowcountry from Central African traditions was the use of *minkisi* (singular form *nkisi*) as vehicles for magic. A nkisi is often depicted in popular literature as a carved wooden figure, usually in an anthropomorphic or animal shape, and was used among the Bakongo people as a way to harness supernatural power with figures that represented the spirit called upon (Anderson 2005: 25–49; Chireau 2003: 46–49; Creel 1988: 57–58; Hyatt 1973; Singleton 1999:118–120; see also Figure 4).

The nkisi figure was traditionally about 12–15 inches tall but could be much taller, and had a hollowed-out stomach cavity in which a combination of powders (ground herbs, roots, leaves, seeds) and other items considered to have magical properties were placed. These were necessary to call a spirit into the nkisi and set a spell into motion. Bits of glass or broken mirror were added to the eyes sometime in the 19th century. Glass was believed to enable the spirit inhabiting the nkisi to see out from the Other World (Wyatt et al. 1993).

Figure 4 Nkisi statuette.

Source: Wikimedia Commons.

Minkisi were traditionally carved from the *Canarium schweinfurthii* Engl.
tree (commonly known as the bush candle, the African olive, the African elemi,
or the canarium tree) of the *Burseraceae* family found in the tropical forests of
the Kongo. The tree has a very dense wood heavy with resin and secretes an
aromatic scent. *Burseraceae* trees are perhaps more well-known historically for
their Old World value in European trade rather than for their sculpting properties – their resins produced frankincense and myrrh, scents "once worth their
weight in gold" and used in incense and perfume in Christian ritual.[7] Other trees
from the *Burseraceae* family were used to carve minkisi statuettes if the
preferred species was not available. There are no trees from the *Burseraceae*
family native to the South Carolina Lowcountry; however, farther south into
Florida there is a relative of the *Burseraceae* family known as the Gumbo
Limbo tree. This tree is also resistant to drought, though its resin scent is not
appealing. Gumbo Limbo tree bark is primarily used as waterproofing varnish;
other medicinal uses include reducing pain and/or itching from insect bites,
sunburn, and sunstroke. The resin and leaves of the tree can also be boiled to

---

[7] Arizona Sonora Desert Museum (ASDM), www.desertmuseum.org/books/nhsd_burseraceae
.php.

make tea to treat gout (Canopy Family 2018). Ultimately, enslaved peoples had to work with the natural resources that were available and so they repurposed European items to which they had access for symbolic use. Carving a statuette would have been difficult to hide.

Pragmatism and necessity guided the choice to transform minkisi from figurines kept in a static place into an innocuous and mobile form – they became lightweight pouches that could be worn on the body, hidden from view, and that had meaningful objects of spiritual and magical importance sewn up inside them. Similar amulets and charms are often referred to as *gris gris, ju-ju, mojo bundles*, or *wangas* in the literature and popular culture, which often conflate them as one and the same (Chireau 2003: 47; Long 2001: 39; Pinckney 2003: 6, 45). However, the terms are historically differentiated: gris gris, ju-ju, and mojo were originally associated with the Louisiana population of enslaved and their practices (New Orleans in particular), while wanga has been associated with a specific purpose (harmful) and is aligned with East African groups (Insoll 2015; Long 2003: 39; Pinckney 2003: 6). For this reason, the author has opted to refer to these objects as *spirit bundles* that can be used in ritual magic deposits, charms, or amulets; it is a more neutral label. Spirit bundles can be related to West and Central African groups (particular to the Lowcountry enslaved population) without attaching them to preconceived concepts linked to other African religions and practices not represented on the Hume Plantation.

The ideology of inhabiting spirits was transferred in principle from a minkisi statuette to a spirit bundle. Pieces of ceramic, shell, and other objects considered to have power were inserted in a pouch along with iron (nails). In this pragmatic shift, the nails were inserted inside instead of being added to the outside, as they once had been on minkisi figurines. Mundane objects or those having a common use-life were preferred since they would not draw unwelcome attention when they were collected for ritual or magical use. Items were frequently bound together with twine and/or sewn inside a cloth pouch (see Figure 5).

Flannel was a relatively cheap fabric and allocated to the enslaved by the yard each year per household. The enslaved were tasked with constructing clothing for themselves (Shaw 2012). Flannel was sturdy and ubiquitous on plantations and among Southerners of lower socioeconomic standing. The heavy woolen material was inexpensive, available in bulk, and came mainly in gray and blue colors, which may also explain its eventual use for the Confederate uniform. In addition, blue was considered by the enslaved to be a color of supernatural and spiritual significance.

Every spirit bundle had a specific purpose and meaning. An individual would approach a conjurer or root doctor to request one constructed to address a specific concern. Some were used for protection – physical or spiritual – and some to promote healing or alleviate troublesome symptoms. Others could be used for

Figure 5 Enslaved woman making a spirit bundle.
Source: Drawing by the author.

vengeance and to cause harm or death and were often buried in a strategic place. Spirit bundles could be worn on a string as a necklace or hidden around the waist, under one's clothing. Others were not worn at all but were ritual deposits buried in the ground to invoke supernatural action.

Ritual magic deposits, their composition and placement, make up the bulk of data on ritual activities in the Hume Plantation slave quarter. Deposits have been found in and around hearths inside the cabin, beneath the floorboards, or buried in the dirt in backyard garden areas and adjacent structures. Some deposits were found under cabin foundation corner timbers or along specific walls that corresponded to a cardinal direction of spiritual significance. Others were buried in what could be considered *liminal* or *transitional spaces*, such as beneath doorways and under windows. Liminal spaces were seen as gateways between the living world and the supernatural world, where spirits of the dead and nature spirits could cross over into the physical realm. These also included waterways – the shoreline, canals, and streams near the slave quarter. Water sources were considered by both Native Americans and Africans to be sacred places. Shells of marine and freshwater origin are the most frequently used material in deposits found on the Hume Plantation.

There are other materials of human, animal, or plant origin that play a role in certain hoodoo practices depending upon the spell's purpose, such as roots, fingernails, fur, hair, bones, animal hide, and bodily fluids. While these things may have been present in a range of conjure work, organic materials would no longer be present in the Hume Plantation deposits. It is for this reason that discussion of the deposits is limited to what survived.

As noted in Section 1.5 on environmental factors, the acidity level of the soils on the Hume slave street was tested and showed a pH of 3–4 on a scale of 0–14, which is considered high. Soils with high acidity are not conducive to preservation of any organic material, even bones. Teeth are an exception because they are not bone but made up of enamel, calcium, phosphorus, and minerals and are thus much more likely to survive in the archaeological record. Likewise, shells are made up of calcium carbonate and will last longer in a high acidity environment.

Hearths held spiritual significance; fire was an element provided by the stars (lightning) in many Native sacred stories. In African sacred lore, certain spirits are attracted to fire and heat and this is useful in ritual deposits meant to call them forth; thus, a number of ritual deposits were found in the floors around the hearths of the cabins (Anderson 2005).

A conjurer would create a spirit bundle at a client's request in exchange for a payment of some kind and call a spirit into it to invoke an intervention. The person for whom the bundle was made was instructed on how and where to place it if a ritual deposit, or how to wear it. Following those instructions, the ritual released the power it contained with proper symbols. Sometimes "wine, saliva, or blood" was used to feed the spirit that inhabited the nkisi or spirit bundle, which was perceived as a living being; this would then energize it and bring about the desired chain of events (Chireau 2003: 49; Long 2001: 97).

3.1 The 21 Hoodoo Deposits

There were twenty-one initially recognizable hoodoo deposits discovered on the Hume Plantation slave street that were placed in specific locations. Most were buried beneath slave cabin floors and associated structures such as sheds, fencing, backyard gardens, and other targeted areas. The majority of the hoodoo deposits appeared to be for protection, for success, or for curative purposes. In one case the deposit seemed to indicate a spell with intent to harm (see Table 3).

Excavated artifacts suggest that some Western ideas about social class had also been adopted among the enslaved over time insomuch as class ideology and social hierarchy were imposed for many years. The enslaved had to learn how to navigate the system that dominated their lives, which then translated into

Table 3 The 21 identified ritual deposits, which reflect an identifiable pattern

Deposit #	Depth	Description	Cabin
#1	Level 3	1 shark tooth w/2 nails; burned	Cabin 3
#2	Level 3	2 square nails w/oyster shell & 2 metal buttons, each of which has a single brass loop, or "eye," on the back, which dates them to 1785–1800	Cabin 4
#3	Level 4	Mirror pieces w/2 nails	Cabin 4
#4	Level 4	A medicine bottle that was ¾ intact w/2 nails and an oyster shell; the bottle would have been cast-off trash from a white doctor's medicinal use, which is likely why it was reused symbolically in a magic deposit – it implies that the spell had a healing purpose.	Cabin 3
#5	Level 4	Native American projectile point Biface w/blue Euro ceramic piece	Cabin 2
#6	Level 4	Glass, blue & white Euro ceramic pieces w/2 nails	Cabin 2
#7	Level 4	Glass, colonoware & 2 nails	Cabin 2
#8	Level 2	Rhyolite projectile point	Overseer House
#9	Level 2	2 nails corroded to white ceramic piece	Cabin 4
#10	Level 2	Oyster shell w/2 nails	Cabin 4
#11	Level 2	Oyster shell 2/medicine bottle piece	Cabin 4
#12	Level 3	White Euro ceramic piece and 2 nails	Cabin 5
#13	Level 3	2 white & 1 blue Euro ceramic pieces w/2 nails	Cabin 5
#14	Level 2	Oyster shell w/white Euro ceramic piece	Cabin 4
#15	Level 3	White Euro ceramic, Native American pottery & 1 nail	Cabin 3
#16	Level 3	7 white Euro ceramic pieces, 2 Colonoware ceramic piece & 3 nails	Cabin 3
#17	Level 3	1 nail, 1 black & 1 white ceramic piece	Cabin 3
#18	Level 3	2 nails crossed and corroded in "X"; w/1 white Euro ceramic piece	Cabin 3
#19	Level 3	White Euro ceramic piece & 2 nails crossed	Backyard of Cabin 3
#20	Level 2	Coral pieces; colonoware pieces and 4 oyster shells	Cabin 3 Shed
#21	Level 3	White Euro ceramic, 2 nails & oyster shell w/1 blue bead	Cabin 3

expressions of social division among themselves that continued after emanci-pation. We can infer this from the different excavation levels that show a continued disparity in the quality of ceramics, personal adornment, and other items that are found in the upper end of the slave street (nearest what was the Main House) compared to those found on the lower end. For those who continued to live temporarily in the slave cabins farther down the slave street, colonoware, a rough pottery made by the enslaved, still characterized much of their household wares and there were fewer personal items. Given that after emancipation many freed individuals had nowhere to go and stayed on, at least for a time, the items of those living on the upper end of the slave street suggest continued differentiation.

This is not to suggest that the notion of social hierarchy was unknown among the enslaved before their enslavement. Social status, wealth, and political power were part of the social fabric among West African tribes before enslavement. Success and symbols of wealth or power were expressed with standardization of value imbued to cowry shells. The cowries were eventually replaced by imported beads when cowries became too attainable for everyone. The scarcity of the manufactured beads raised their monetary and symbolic value and they eventually replaced the cowry shell (Ogundiran 2002: 448).

Certain artifacts and repurposed European materials in ritual/magic deposits indicate controlled access to certain wares during enslavement. Inhabitants of the cabins closest to the Main House were afforded more hand-me-downs from the plantation owner and other small privileges. At the Hume Plantation it is likely that a conjurer resided in the upper half of the slave street, based upon the collection of special deposits and repurposed upper-class materials found around Cabins 2 and 3. Surprisingly, very little was found around Cabin 1 and it appeared almost vacant or perhaps had one occupant, judging by the minimal amount of refuse in the trash pit and other signs of active inhabitation.

Evidence suggests that, alternately, enslaved families that lived farthest away from the Main House were also those with the least social status and whose value was their field labor. There is not much to suggest any meaningful interaction with the Main House residents. While colonoware was found throughout the slave street, the highest concentrations of it were found in the lower half, namely Cabins 5, 6, and 7 (Cabin 8 had limited excavation and produced very little).

The four lower cabins revealed the fewest and most utilitarian household items compared to the upper half of the slave street. While there was some evidence of ritual deposits found among those four cabins, these were limited in scope and purpose – and appear to have been primarily for protective purposes or to benefit an individual or the family. Other deposits in the backyard or garden areas suggest requests for growth, success, or to keep boundaries from being breached by negative forces, including interference from neighbors. The interpretations are general and based upon the placement and content of oyster shells, nails (for power to invoke), and colors in white and blue that symbolize water and deities and/or ancestors, and can be inferred to bring positive aspects. More about color symbolism and associations with water elements will be discussed in Section 3.4.

Hoodoo deposits were mainly conglomerated around the upper four cabins of the slave street on the east side. Unfortunately, three additional slave cabins along the west side – Cabins 9, 10, and 11 – were located in front of the cattle pen and livestock stalls and were not excavated within the time frame of the Hume Plantation Project. This was mainly due to thick tree growth, as opposed to the east side which had limited tree growth and limited time and funds to compensate for the additional labor needed to clear the area. Partial excavation was possible on a corner of the Overseer's House on the west side: there was a slight clearing, which was enough to expose access to the northwest corner (see the Figure 3 plat map).

The Reconstruction phase of the post–Civil War era offered little to emancipated African Americans, though county records indicate that those who stayed on were laborers for plantations struggling to keep their rice production viable. Emancipated individuals who stayed continued to live in their previous slave cabins in subpar conditions, with no running water or electricity, and barely maintained a living wage to feed themselves. Medical needs were still largely addressed by conjurers, as they had been during the enslavement period. Common ailments claimed African American lives due to poor conditions and malnourishment. The post–Civil War years into the 20th century saw many of the emancipated fleeing to the American North or simply to other places to establish their own communities as free people. However, there were some who chose to stay on the plantation and continue as paid workers (although the pay was minimal or nonexistent in exchange for a place to live), having too few resources, poor health, older age, or family connections that discouraged them from moving on. Conjurers who stayed still had influence and filled a need among the black population, as they continued to address health problems that white doctors couldn't or wouldn't attend to. White resistance to the Reconstruction contributed to the ongoing instability of the South for both the black and the white populations. In this context, conjure magic remained an important part of African American lives as it filled a void in assuaging anxieties and fears experienced by the black population.

In 1850 approximately 500 enslaved Africans were residing on the plantations on Cat and South Islands; by 1860 in Georgetown County, South Carolina the enslaved African population was over 18,000 compared to the white population of approximately 3,000.[8] By the 1930s, during the Great Depression years, that number had dwindled to fewer than 100 African Americans in residence (Giauque et al. 2010: 16).

3.2 Objects of Power and Magic at the Hume Plantation

Spirit bundles and magic charms were by necessity small and could be worn without being visible to others. Objects of power for invoking spirits were easily gathered and/or repurposed, including cast-off European materials such as ceramics, metals, fabrics, and so on. Native American and African botanical and other organic resources such as roots and bodily fluids would not survive in the archaeological record, though prehistoric objects such as projectile points, lithics, and Native pottery and basic marine and freshwater resources were also accessible.

Many of these were considered mundane objects that were used or consumed in the daily lives of the enslaved. Occasionally, other specialty items were repurposed, such as beads, buttons, and other pieces of iron and metal. The following is an itemization and explanation of the symbolism of objects used in ritual/magic deposits on the Hume Plantation. In addition, there are some items that didn't fall into clearly identified categories of magic practice because their composition was unique or the sample was too small to ascertain a pattern. They are noted because their composition may suggest other known symbolisms and their placement suggests special meaning and purposeful treatment that deserve attention.

Hoodoo magic was guided by color and material symbols that were aligned with the elements: water, air, fire, and earth. Cosmograms incorporated the four aspects of existence – birth, life, death, and rebirth – and a spell was ritually put into motion based upon one of the four prescribed times of day – sunrise, noon, sunset, or midnight – also known as the "four moments of the sun" (Long 2001: 55; Thompson 1981; Wassie 2021). Thus, placement beneath the floor near a hearth (fire source) or in a particular corner of a foundation or yard held meaning (see Table 4).

3.3 Colonoware

There was an abundance of *colonoware* excavated among the cabin sites in the Hume slave quarter. In all excavation seasons save for one that focused on other areas of the slave street, colonoware accounted for some of the most significant amounts of ceramic finds numbering into several hundred per season. Because the incidence rate of the material was comparatively higher than other ceramic

---

[8] NARA, 1860 Census Records, www.archives.gov/research/census/1860 (accessed September 19, 2024).

Table 4 Cabins and unit locations

East side of street	
Cabin	**Units**
One	Units 1, 9, 20, 21, 22
	Unit 25 at boundary between Cabins 1 and 2
Two	Units 2, 11, 12, 14, 23, 24, 29
	Unit 3 at boundary between Cabins 2 and 3
Three	Units 4, 10, 15, 27B, 27C, 27D, 28, 33
Driver's House	Unit 26 – northeast corner of shed in backyard
Four	Units 5, 16A, 18, 19, 27, 27A, 34
	Unit 6 at boundary between Cabins 4 and 5
Five	Units 17, 35, 36, 38
Six	Units 34 (early closeout due to tree roots), 37, 39
Seven	Unit 32; extensive root interference; no further units
	Unit 8 at boundary between Cabins 7 and 8
Eight	Units 7, 30, 31
West side of street	
Cabin	
Overseer's House	(Parallel to the east side/Cabins 4 and 5 across the street)
	Unit 13 – corner post stain

types and seemed concentrated among the slave cabins, particularly those on the lower end of the slave street, it suggests that the colonoware was produced onsite on the Hume Plantation rather than traded from Natives, and that its purpose was mainly everyday use. Resource materials were abundant on Cat Island (clay, sand, temper materials).

Colonoware is an unglazed, handmade, and quickly produced earthenware pottery, usually made for utilitarian purposes and composed of local clays with sand or shell temper. As an unglazed ceramic it was easily replaced when cracked or broken; its use-life was typically short. Poor or inconsistent firing techniques indicate an open fire rather than firing in a kiln, and fracture patterns suggest quick processing. Enslaved crafters on the Hume Plantation would not have had access to a kiln and the resources necessary to properly maintain a fire in one. Instead, it is likely that they used their hearths or their yards' open fire pits for this purpose. To be clear, colonoware was not a favored ceramic by the enslaved. Rather, it was produced out of necessity and easy access to local resources (Ferguson 1992; Singleton 1999).

Many of the enslaved on the Hume Plantation were from West Africa and sought-after because of their familiarity with and knowledge of rice planting and harvesting. Their homeland was geographically similar to Cat Island, with its marshes and ocean to freshwater estuaries, sand, clay, silty soils, and an abundance of shells that could be used for temper. West and Central African ceramics are well decorated and identifiable – but colonoware remained undecorated for the majority of its utilitarian and short use-life. It is clear that this pottery type was unlikely to have been produced as a trade item by Natives who made finer wares for their aesthetic and trade appeal. The vast amount of colonoware at any enslaved site indicates that it was made locally and by the people that used it, to be thrown away and quickly replaced.

Colonoware sherds were found all around the Hume slave cabins, usually in middens (i.e., trash pits). Occasionally, colonoware sherds were found in the earthen floors of the cabins and regarded as cast-off debris. It is only when the sherds were found in an identifiable patterned deposit associated with other recognizable ritual materials that they were regarded as ritualized objects.

Some colonoware found in South Carolina was considered similar to the ceramics found in West and Central African archaeological sites because of its construction. This suggests that crafter(s) may have followed established knowledge of ceramic technology, which they brought with them to North America (Polhemus 1977).

Early arguments that the enslaved traded their garden produce and other items at their disposal to acquire colono-Indian ware from friendly Native groups for everyday use have been challenged (Ferguson 1992). This is because most tradeworthy ceramics produced by Natives were made of finer clays using mica, quartz, and finer tempers, and using different ceramic techniques. Native specialty wares were also traded to European settlers. Most whites, even among the lower socioeconomic group, would have been able to acquire Native-made ceramics. This is not to say that the enslaved did not occasionally trade for Native ceramics too; however, those trade items were more likely viewed as decorative and used on a more limited basis than for everyday cooking, food storage, or food preparation. Colonoware was a simple pottery and tended to be coarse and bulky.

Later, burnishing colonoware became a way to improve its aesthetics; it gave the impression of more sophistication by imitating finer European ceramics such as porcelain (Ferguson 1992). Another argument for Hume Plantation colonoware originating from within the enslaved population was the proliferation of sherds from spherical vessels: bowls, tureens, and lids, or other curved surfaces. West and Central African cultural dishware displays a preference for bowls and curved vessels (pitchers, jugs, crocks, cisterns) as the norm (Ferguson 1992: 96–107). Flat plates and platters were quite rare among the enslaved. When found among enslaved living spaces, it is because they were acquired as hand-me-downs from their European masters.

3.3.1 The "X" Symbolism

In addition to the everyday use of colonoware, there are also contexts that indicate its crossover use in ritual activities in some enslaved sites, though this was not proven at the Hume Plantation. An "X" incised into the bottom of colonoware vessels has been found in several places in the South (Ferguson 1992). The "X" symbol is associated with Bakongo cosmograms (Joseph 1989; Russell 1997).

There is not enough information to determine exactly how the ritually marked objects were used, but the "X," according to known Bakongo spiritual beliefs, stood for the four realms of the spiritual plane and belief in the immortality and reincarnation of the Bakongo soul. In this belief system, the soul could return in human form but could also appear as part of Nature's landscapes (Thompson 1983). This is very similar to the regard for the sacred cardinal directions in Native American spirituality and the belief that, besides human beings, inanimate objects such as stones, trees, rivers, and other landscape features are regarded as being alive and having a soul. A synthesis of the two belief systems with regard to perceptions of the spirit world would have been a natural development.

The "X" mark has also been found incised with a sharp implement on repurposed European objects such as spoons, ceramics, buttons, and fired colonoware. The mark was imprinted with a tool into wet, pre-fired colonoware. The "X" mark has been documented on plantations in a wide geographic range of states including Florida, Maryland, South Carolina, Tennessee, Texas, and Virginia, to name but a few (Davidson 2015; Ferguson 1992; Joseph 2011; Russell 1997).

3.3.2 An "X" on Hume Plantation Colonoware?

Among the hundreds of colonoware sherds found on the Hume Plantation, there is only one example of a sherd with a possible "X" incised on it. The mark is incomplete since a lower quarter of it was broken off. The piece came from a Level 2 context (mid 19th century), in Unit 16B. Unit 16B was in a boundary or "liminal" area between Cabins 6 and 7 on the more distant (away from the Main House) end of the slave street and is separate from the twenty-one ritual deposits identified through pattern. The clay is the typical reddish-brown found on the plantation grounds and the sherd appears to come from the bottom of a vessel. It was found in the context of ten other sherds, some of which had been fire blackened. These do not represent the whole vessel and no other pieces were found that would have made reconstruction possible. Ceramic petrography was not completed due to there being only a single sample and due to its incompleteness. It was determined that an in-depth laboratory analysis of this partial piece would not be warranted unless other pieces with "X" marks were found.

The deposit was notable, though, because the eleven pieces were all buried together in one event rather than spread out as inadvertent cast-offs or refuse within a general area. In addition, they were placed in a deposit positioned at the boundary between two cabins where there was evidence of a fence line, indicated by the small-diameter post stains of approximately 7 centimeters (less than 4 inches) that were commonly associated with fenced-in backyard garden areas. The deposit would have been consciously chosen, as it would have required digging around the fence line to accommodate it. Were the sherds simply the mundane remains of a broken vessel, they would have been much more conveniently disposed of in the refuse pit.

Ritual use of colonoware often included pouring liquids in a ritual context and/or preparing hoodoo ingredients over a fire or storing materials. Other researchers have posited that the "X" mark found on some colonoware at other sites can be attributed as a maker's or owner's mark by enslaved potters who could not write their names. Most notably, "Dave the Potter" from Edgefield, South Carolina is known to have signed his pottery with an "X," progressing to signing "Dave," and eventually including short rhyming comments as his stamp of identity and authenticity on his colonoware vessels over 200 miles west of Georgetown/Hume Plantation (Joseph 2011).

Other "X"-marked pots have been found around the Cooper River, South Carolina, which is approximately 60 miles southwest of Georgetown/Hume Plantation (Ferguson 1992: 27). The likelihood of colonoware being traded between these disparate South Carolina locations is minimal, since there would have been no incentive to trade items regularly produced at home. One incidence of an "X"-marked colonoware sherd is not sufficient to draw a conclusion about its possible ritual use, even though the contextual circumstances suggest purposeful burial that sets it apart from general refuse. Instead of incised "X" marks on colonoware, it was far more common on the Hume Plantation to find two nails crossed in an "X" configuration and included with or on top of a ritual deposit (see Figure 11).

There are three ritual deposits among the twenty-one that included colonoware. These were in Units 27B and 27D (Cabin 3) and Unit 12 (Cabin 2). Of these three, only one had the stand-alone sherd with a possible "X" mark.

Iron (to be discussed in Section 3.6) and earthenware were common materials used in house charms and shrines; colonoware pieces found in some ritual deposits suggest that it was also used for this purpose (Davidson 2015: 100–101). House charms were usually buried in the floor, in the foundation corners, and near doorways and windows. Their purpose was to protect the house from evil forces. Installing a house charm often required a sacrifice as well, usually a white bird or a chicken (Parrinder 1969: 161–162).

3.4 Beads and Color Symbolism

There were five colored glass beads found in the Hume Plantation slave quarter. Though a small sample, they date to between the 18th and the early 19th centuries; were found in different stratigraphic levels, indicating different time periods; and were found in only two colors: blue and yellow/amber. The beads were in three different cabin contexts, suggesting different ownerships and possible insight into the color symbolism or value of beads in three different time periods: (1) in the pre-plantation era of Cat Island – among Native Americans likely when Gaillard operated a trading post; (2) during the plantation eras, among the enslaved Africans; and (3) in the emancipation era, among those populations. One cobalt-blue bead (the oldest bead example) was associated with a ritual deposit in Cabin 3, which was the Driver's House (see Table 3).

The driver was normally one of the enslaved who was entrusted with driving the plantation owner's carriage and oversaw the horses and stable equipment. The Driver's House was also notably different compared to all the other "Negro houses" depicted on the hand-drawn plat map (see Figure 3). The house was divided lengthwise by a north–south wall and is the only one configured that way in the slave quarter. Objects associated with horse tack were found in the east side of the divided cabin, which suggests the possibility that a portion of the house was used as a specialty workspace for the driver. Items such as metal buckles used on horse bridles; pieces of a bridle bit; awls for leatherworking and repair to saddles, bridles, and other riding equipment; and part of an axle (carriage) were found in that space.

As stated in Section 2, Bartholomew Gaillard operated a trading post in Jamestown, approximately 25 miles away from the Hume Plantation, over a century earlier than the plantation itself was established. Gaillard was also a property owner on what became South Island, adjacent to Cat Island. It is feasible that Gaillard could have been the original source for the oldest blue-glass trade bead found on the Hume Plantation slave street.

An archaeological relative dating method was used to determine the age of the beads, where comparative analysis was carried out based upon the size, hue, shape, design, and manufacture technology of the known trade bead types found in the American Southeast (see Table 1). This analysis was done in concert with excavation levels for a chronological range and included any association between and among other artifacts found within the same stratigraphic level that provided additional context. There were several archaeological reference materials consulted in dating the beads (Blair et al. 2009; Eddins 2024; Marshall 2012: 189–205; Ogundiran 2002; Russell 1997: 68–71; Stine et al. 1996; Trinkley 1990).

Below is a discussion of four colors and what they symbolize in African hoodoo and ritual practices; this is a limited list of the colors most frequently found in the ritual deposits on the Hume Plantation. They create a pattern of color use and practice. Other colors with symbolic meaning in African culture include but are not limited to red, green, pink/purple, and brown, but these did not appear in the ritual deposits (Stine et al. 1996; Wassie 2021). The range of color symbolisms possible for multiple West African tribes that populated the Lowcountry goes beyond the scope of this Element; thus, while it is acknowledged, it is not extensively discussed. Discussions are limited to those colors that, by pattern of use and quantity, directly contribute to understanding the ritual objects on the Hume slave street.

3.4.1 Blue

In African Bakongo cosmology, blue represents a connection to water: springs, rivers, and other water sources that were perceived as liminal gateways through which spirits could cross from the spiritual world into the human world. Osun is one of the most powerful orishas (goddesses) in Yoruba beliefs and is specifically associated with water (Murphy and Sanford 2001). Blue was also considered a protective color by the enslaved groups brought in from West Africa and used to ward away evil spirits and others who would do harm (Russell 1997: 63–80).

In the mid 17th century, the British had acquired through conquest many Spanish plantations in the Carolinas that produced indigo (Sharrer 1971). By the 1760–1770s, the area known as Georgetown County today, which included Cat Island, was a producer and exporter of indigo as the main cash crop (Butler 2019). This was later replaced by rice production by the time the Hume Plantation was established in the late 18th/early 19th centuries. It is notable in context of the early enslaved populations of Cat Island because indigo was also an important blue dye cultivated in West Africa from which many of them originated; access to plants that could produce indigo may have been an important factor before other European materials, such as ceramic pieces, could be substituted to represent the color in ritual and magic spirit bundles.

From the post–Civil War period into the early 20th century, blue was a commonly chosen paint color for doors and windows among the freed Africans. Islamic religious significance attached to the color blue, or blue-green, had influenced West African spiritual perspectives from as early as the 10th century via contact with Middle Eastern traders and others who observe the Islamic faith in the Ghana region of West Africa. Blue was also linked to the Middle Eastern blue eye charm commonly used to ward off the "evil eye"

(Lapidus 2002). Blue is used to call upon spirits for medicinal reasons as well – mainly as a pain reliever (Creel 1988; Pollitzer 2005). Roman Catholic use of candles in prayer attached to color symbolism and the conflation of saints with African spirits is most evident in Louisiana, but some of the color symbolisms are found in the Lowcountry as well (Creel 1988: 38–39, 51–52; Long 2001: 55–56).

Blue symbolism evolved as representative of the sky and "heaven" by the 20th century and biblical references were added in. Blue was a means to keep out unwanted spirits who then feared the color as a symbol of a Christian heaven (Creel 1988; Heath 1999; Ogundiran 2002; Stine et al. 1996). In contemporary times, it is common to see "bottle trees" with blue-colored bottles hanging from their branches standing as a protective symbol in many rural Southern yards (Rushing 2011; Stine et al. 1996: 63–64). The intent of the trees is to ward off evil from the household and/or to capture evil spirits in the blue bottles. The premise is somewhat similar to some Native American concepts of the purpose of a dreamcatcher.

3.4.2 Yellow/Amber/Gold

Yellow, amber, and gold hues also seem to have special significance as charm elements. Yellow was an important color for invoking healing powers and to protect against harm (Davidson 2015: 104; Stine et al. 1996). The magical efficacy of yellow in the form of amber beads can be traced back to antiquity, when amber was a scarce and prized material mentioned in the writings of Pliny the Elder, as noted by Opie and Tatum (1989: 1): "wearing necklaces of amber, principally as an ornament ... but ... [mindful] of its remedial virtues as well ... It is beneficial for infants also, attached to the body in the form of an amulet."

There are accounts dating from the mid 19th century attesting to the high value that West African tribes in the region of Sierra Leone placed upon amber, amber-colored glass, and agates (Thomson 1846: 132). There is an account in the early 20th century of a single bead being used in an animal sacrifice (a hen) in the context of ceremony around a funeral, but the bead color was not noted (Thomas 1917: 170).

During the trade bead era, Native Americans sewed beads on clothing and other articles not only for aesthetic purposes but also as an expression of spiritual significance, which they attached to certain colors. A common theme in native spirituality is that four different colors are associated with the cardinal directions, and the power of the spirits and the natural elements is connected to those directions. Of course, there are tribal differences. We do not have a consensus of accepted interpretation for Catawba, Waccamaw, or other

Southeastern tribal color values for the period spanning the 17th and 18th centuries because such details were rarely noted in European historical accounts. During that time, the emphasis among the Spanish and the British was on building military alliances with select Native groups to further their own advantage or exploiting Indigenous captives for slave trading (Gallay 2002). Trading posts usually carried trade beads for Native customers and the military used beads when negotiating with Native allies, to foster goodwill. Ethnographic accounts of spiritual details are sparse, and traditions passed down among Southeastern Indigenous groups were fractured due to war, disease, relocation, and reconfiguring of tribal identities, as tribes coalesced with neighboring groups for survival.

Examination of four glass beads excavated on the Hume slave street, using bead charts and comparative analysis of production style, suggests that two beads date from the mid 1700s. The four beads were found in 19th to 20th-century levels and associated with materials also dating from that period (Marcoux 2012).

This suggests either that the older beads were acquired by Natives and then secondarily acquired and repurposed by the enslaved African population, or that the enslaved acquired the beads through other means and selectively chose certain colors that matched African color values (Stine et al. 1996). Although the sample is small, the beads were either yellow/amber/gold or blue hued to the exclusion of all other colors. In a Native American context, one would expect to find an assortment of trade bead colors; beads were colorful adornments on clothing and other items as well as being used for symbolic purposes. African ritual color choices are, therefore, suggested by the limited palette. The beads were spread out between three different cabins.

Of the four beads, two were yellow and two were blue hued. The two faceted yellow beads dated from the mid to late 19th century – the Victorian era – and were matched to the Munsell Bead color system chart with a hue rating of 2.5Y 7/8 – light gold hue. One each was found in the flooring of Cabins 2 and 4.

Of the two blue beads, both were found in association with Cabin 3 (Driver's House) but only one was placed in a ritual deposit. This consisted of the single bead (blue) stacked together with two oyster shells, a piece of European white-ware, and two hand-cut square nails bound in an "X" configuration that were placed directly on top (see Figures 6 and 7); this ritual deposit was in the southeast corner of the Driver's House. The stratigraphic level and assessment of the nails' manufacture technology dated the deposit to the mid 19th century, approximately the Civil War era. The blue bead was much older than the other objects in the deposit. Both blue beads were color matched using the Munsell Color system with a rating of 7.5PB 2/10 – royal blue – and were in the purple blue end of the spectrum.

Figure 6 Blue bead from ritual deposit.

Source: Photo by the author.

Figure 7 Crossed nails from a ritual deposit – corroded.

Source: Photo by the author.

3.4.3 White

In terms of symbolic meaning, "white" in Western African rituals and magical constructions is associated with a number of concepts including peace, purity, the ancestors, rebirth, compassion, and justice (Long 2001: 56; Stine et al. 1996: 53–56). It is used toward invoking the power of spirits and deities equated with water, as the sources of the white color used in many instances are shells. This is particularly so in the Lowcountry; white is the most prolific color represented by objects in ritual/magic deposits on the Hume Plantation slave street.

3.4.4 Black

Black in hoodoo symbolism is often expressed with black hen's feathers or stones, and has been associated with black magic or witchcraft; it is an important color for the invocation of harm and curses. A black ceramic piece was present in one spirit bundle deposit on the Hume Plantation. It was located in the backyard near the shed of Cabin 3, the Driver's House.

Black was historically the main color in Adinkra cloth in traditional Ghanaian culture and associated with mourning, memorials, and funerals (Wassie 2021). Alternatively, black was also used in counterspells to combat black magic that had been used against someone or their household (Chireau 2003: 74–77; Long 2001).

3.5 Shells: Water and Protection Symbolism

Historically, West African peoples' use of cowry shells began as a form of currency and to display wealth. Besides being used in market exchange and other transactions, the shells were also used to decorate homes and as personal adornment. This was most notable in the Yoruba region of West Africa. In some instances, oyster shells were used as jewelry grave goods for infants as a status symbol (Insoll 2015: 63). Cowries could also be used as visual cues to signal the family's hierarchal place in society. Cowries in this context were worn in the 18th century to demonstrate political power by the wearer and thus helped maintain political influence by select families (Gregory 1996: 195; Haour 2019; Ogundiran 2002: 446).

For this Element, the relevance of cowry shells to West African groups before enslavement is in their ritual contexts and influences toward finding substitution shells in the South Carolina Lowcountry. Cowry shells are not native to or found along the South Carolina coastline or the American Southeast. The closest sites where one might find cowry shells in North America are the central to southern coast of California, parts of Mexico, and southward into South America

(Hogendorn and Johnson 1986). Trade for cowries would have been improbable among the Lowcountry enslaved who would have had little to no interaction with trade routes and groups that had access to them, and as cowries were an expensive resource, they would have had little means to procure them even if they had had interactions.

It is believed that ritual use of cowries likely began sometime after the 16th century in West Africa due to the abundance of them and the easy access to them by trade (Ogundiran 2002: 448). Cowries became associated with construction of home altars and shrines used in magic practice and ritual. However, as the cowry shells became common, they slowly lost some of their status value and those who held higher political and/or socioeconomic positions began to use beads in the construction of their altars and shrines instead. Beads were scarce and required more influence to acquire; different bead colors also had an impact on availability and price (Drewel and Mason 1998: 17–20).

Cowries were used for divination, in protective spells, and to facilitate contact with ancestral spirits besides the pantheon of gods and goddesses from whom protection and/or guidance were sought. Because cowries held such an important role, the enslaved continued to view the symbolic importance of shells as something that could not be overlooked. It is in this context that the archaeological evidence at the Hume Plantation suggests that oyster shells became a substitute in lieu of the traditional cowry shells.

Of the twenty-one recognizable ritual deposits found on the Hume slave street, seven included white oyster shells as part of a multiple-piece deposit. All of the object deposits combined with shells were found in association with Cabins 3 and 4 (see Table 4).

There is a pattern of two or more shells being bundled together with other items. Time and the decomposition of cloth and most organic materials have left only the shells, nails, and other man-made or bone objects intact. Sometimes iron objects corroded together that were once tightly bound. Water symbolism was significant as representing a place of entrance from the spiritual into the living world for spirits and considered a blessing substance (Chireau 2003; Insoll 2015: 132–133). This fit well with the concept of Christian baptism that had been adopted by converted African Americans. Assimilation and transference of this practice posed no conflict for the enslaved, who already believed in the blessings that water could bestow (Chireau 2003: 53–54; Creel 1988: 293–295).

3.6 Nails and Iron Symbolism

Two or more nails being included in a bundle with shells or other objects and bound in the shape of an "X" was one of the most consistent ritual practices discovered in the Hume Plantation slave quarter (see Figure 7). Sixteen of the twenty-one deposits included nails that were either originally bound into the shape of an "X" or had been included in the ritual bundle, where some had corroded onto other objects in the bundle over time. These constructions were found in deposits from the top of the slave street beginning with Cabin 2, closest to the Main House, and in association with Cabins 3, 4, and 5 out of the eight cabins represented on the east side of the slave street.

Earliest nail samples were hand-cut square nails (see Figure 8). The manufacture process indicates that the nails were produced in the late 18th to the early 19th centuries (1780s–1830).

The levels of stratigraphy in which the deposits were found establish a timeline. By the later half of the 19th century, nail-inclusive deposits have waned and there are only two examples, indicating a shift in spell types on the slave street.

The carved wooden anthropomorphic minkisi figures from West and Central Africa were distinguished by nails that were driven into the body of the statuette (see Figure 4). The use of iron nails was to infuse the figure with power and to invoke the spirit to carry out the spell. Nail fetishes were particular to the Kongo (Chireau 2003: 47). The more iron pieces inserted, the more power infused into the figure to engage the spirit. Nails could sometimes also be used to indicate the number of times a spirit had been called upon. Minkisi were used for a variety of purposes from protection and curing to witchcraft/cursing and revenge. When used by innocent and wronged individuals to exact vengeance on a wrongdoer, the practice was considered not as an evil act associated with black magic but as a "justice" spell that was warranted. The iron of the nail was considered

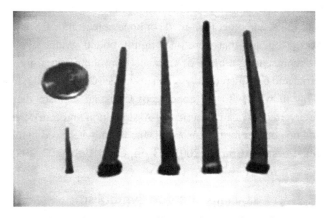

Figure 8 Handcut square nails – 18th to early 19th century.
Source: Wikimedia Commons.

a supernatural conduit that could be used in several ways (Bassani 1977: 36–40; Bockie 1993: 40–66; Chireau 2003: 47; Davidson 2015: 103–105).

Iron and iron concretions known as laterite were naturally occurring in the soils of West Africa. Tribes of the region, such as the Yoruba, the Ibo, and the Dagomba, considered certain stones, including laterite, to have meaning and spiritual power within them (Davidson 2015: 103–104). Blacksmithing and iron-working skills were known among West African tribes, but they came at a price since iron was considered very powerful and required sacrifice when collected: "iron concretions or laterites . . . were historically used by black-smiths in the pre-colonial era as raw ore for iron smelting . . . laterites were considered dangerous . . . a sacrifice had to be performed" (Njoku 1991: 205).

Europeans and non-African peoples historically misunderstood this original practice of hammering the iron nails into the minkisi as an example of sympa-thetic magic. The commodification of the so-called voodoo doll in contemporary sales to tourists further promotes this misunderstood interpretation of the nails. Modern voodoo dolls replace nails with pins and are sold in kits or as ready-made souvenirs (Long 2001: 154; see Figure 9). This is not to suggest that conjurers did not practice sympathetic magic for harm, but with regard to the appropriated ideology of minkisi statuettes, the voodoo doll was a commercialized object that exploited a popular misconception.

Minkisi figures were intended to keep social order in check, either with positive magic or by black magic hex. The *nkondi* version of the minkisi (the nailed figures) was specifically designed as an aggressive vessel meant for harm, revenge, cruelty, or personal gain (MacGaffey 2000: 100–101; see Figure 4).

Nails were found in deposits located in the northeast and southwest founda-tion corners of the cabins and along the west (street-facing) walls. Cabin 3 had a significant number of nail-inclusive ritual deposits (five) that had been placed beneath the foundation framework of a shed in the backyard; these were placed equidistantly from each other. The shed was likely positioned near a garden area, based upon neighboring cabins that fenced in their gardens. Four of the five deposits included two oyster shells and/or sherd(s) of repurposed European white or blue ceramic.

3.7 European Ceramics: Repurposed Sherds

Eleven of the twenty-one ritual deposits contained sherd(s) of European ceram-ics: whiteware or pearlware. Three of the deposits also contained ceramic sherds that were blue (painted or with blue transferware patterns). Most deposits con-taining ceramics included one to two sherds. The significance of blue has already been discussed for its association with water, sky/heaven, and protective

Figure 9 Commercial voodoo doll.
Source: Author's collection.

properties (see Section 3.4.1). In only two examples are both an oyster shell and a piece of white European ceramic ware included in the deposit. Since they are both white materials, utilizing both suggests that there was a differentiated symbolic intention for their inclusion in those two deposits. Perhaps white ceramic pieces were included with white oyster shells as symbolic of the color of purity, while the white oyster shell was symbolic of the water spirits and protection.

There were many different types of imported ceramic found on the Hume Plantation that reflect different historical periods, varying quality/quantity, and approximate dates when they were known to be imported from Europe and Great Britain to North America. The vast ceramic typologies are too numerous to list here, and aside from their context in ritual deposits and symbolic meaning, their relevance outside of ritual/magic deposits is limited to establishing a time frame (see Figure 10).

Table 5 shows a limited selection of ceramic pattern examples most frequently found and highest in quantity from field seasons 2011–2012 when the bulk were excavated. Dating of the ceramic examples found specifically on the slave street is based upon production technology combined with dates when the ceramic types were known to have been imported into the colonies and/or the postcolonial era in the American Southeast. The majority of the ceramic pieces did not have

Table 5 European ceramic types on the Hume Plantation

Ceramic type	Quantity	Historical era	Production dates
Whiteware	230	Postcolonial	1820–1900
Pearlware	171	Postcolonial	1785–1840
Transferware prints	61	Colonial to postcolonial	1770s–1860s
Hand-painted patterns	50	Colonial to postcolonial	1700s–1830
Creamware	47	Colonial to postcolonial	1770–1825
Decal patterns (dots)	6	Postcolonial	1830–1870

Figure 10 European ceramic sherd examples.
Source: Photo by the author.

a surviving maker's mark for more specific identification, so a more generalized diagnostic technique and median dates for them were applied (Fontana 1970; Maryland Archaeological Conservation Lab [MACL] 2002; Miller 1993; Mullins et al. 2013; Nash 2009; Shepherd 2014).

3.8 Buttons

There were forty-five buttons of various sorts excavated among the "Negro houses" identified on the plat map of the slave street. Of those, two metal buttons with single brass eye-loop attachments on the back date from 1785–1800, and were found in a ritual deposit in Cabin 4. The single brass eye-loop buttons were mass produced during the post–Revolutionary War period, also known as the Confederation period – a time of transition for the fledgling United States (Ferling 2004).

The deposit was found below the west wall of Cabin 4 (street-facing) and below a window – which can be construed as a "liminal" area. The buttons were

included in a bundle with two square nails and an oyster shell. Another button
was placed in Level 3, at the foundation level of the cabin, and coincided with
the late 18th-century date as provided by the diagnostic on the button manufacture style (Olson 1963).

The remaining forty-three buttons were found in contexts that did not appear
to indicate ritual. They were found throughout the slave quarter and were made
of various materials: metal, glass, and ceramic. The oldest button was molded
with a seam and a single wire loop for attachment on its back. Its construction
dated it to 1760–1790 and only half of the button was recovered from Cabin 5
(Olson 1963).

3.9 Native American Lithics: Repurposed

There were two instances of Native prehistoric lithics that had been repurposed
for a ritual deposit. The first was found in the foundation of the northwest corner
of Cabin 2. The biface, probably originally used as a scraper, was mostly intact,
with one bottom corner broken off, and deposited with a blue European ceramic
sherd. Its level of deposition indicates that it is one of the earliest cabins
constructed on the slave street and prior to the property's establishment as the
Hume Plantation. As property ownership and exact dates are problematical due to
loss of county records because of the Civil War, it is estimated that perhaps the
earlier incarnation of the slave street was during the time of indigo cultivation.

The second instance was a repurposed Native rhyolite projectile point that
was deposited in the northwest corner of the Overseer's House on the west side
of the slave street. This is one of the few structures partially excavated on the
west side of the street, due to thick tree growth and underbrush. The projectile
point was placed at the top of a square foundation post, as evidenced by the
intact square post stain and the neatly laid projectile point on top of it.

It is unclear what the interpretation for this deposit may have been. It may
have represented strength or aggression. Other uses of prehistoric articles such
as Native American projectile points included in charm bundles were for their
"intrinsic talismanic value" or the "ritual production of sparks" (Russell 1997:
73). Repurposed chert projectile points were placed in deposits at the Hermitage
Plantation in Tennessee and thought to symbolically represent spark-strikers
(Russell 1997: 74).

3.10 Medicinal Glass Bottles: Repurposed

There are two cases of remnant medicinal glass bottles being included in ritual
deposits. The first was a partial bottle included with two nails and an oyster shell
associated with the southeast corner of Cabin 3, and a second partial bottle was

associated with a Cabin 4 deposit placed along the west wall (street-facing). Both bottles were of clear glass that had a faint aqua tinge.

The medicine they contained has not been definitively identified, but the bottles were recognizable as to type and design as being associated with European liniments or embrocation used for sore muscles and joints. Most of the enslaved relied upon their own conjurers and root doctors to provide treatments and salves for their illnesses and injuries; they did not trust in the white doctors as a rule. Plantation owners were also hesitant to obtain and pay for white doctors to treat the everyday maladies of their slaves unless they were quite severe and the investment in the cost of the slave dictated that they were "worth" the expense to save rather than replace.

However, for the enslaved individuals that had more contact with the Main House and the plantation owner's family, such as the driver and/or, presumably, the enslaved persons in Cabins 1, 2, 3 (Driver's House), and possibly Cabin 4, it is likely that they would have had medicines administered to them that the majority of the enslaved did not. Enslaved persons in the cabins closest to the Main House would have had more interactions with the owner and his family than with the rest of the enslaved population. For this reason, the owner may have been more forthcoming with simple medicines and salves for them than for the rest of the enslaved population. We can see other examples of cast-off or hand-me-down wares in the possession of the enslaved in the upper end of the slave quarter that were not found in the cabins lower on the slave street, indicating more access and a hierarchy of privilege afforded to certain enslaved individuals.

Calomel lotion to treat malaria is another possible content of some cast-off bottles. Calomel was usually packaged in yellow or brownish glass apothecary bottles rather than the aqua glass found, however. Cat Island was swampy and humid, and it is common knowledge that most plantation owners avoided their Lowcountry plantations during the summer months when malaria was a concern. As a rule, darker glass bottles were used to protect contents from degrading ultraviolet light, but contents could be packaged in aqua or clear glass bottles if in white powder or tablet form (Kang and Pedersen 2017). Calomel was used for a wide scope of ailments besides malaria: constipation, influenza, parasites, and syphilis. Its mercury content was the main active ingredient, but it also led to mercury poisoning that could result in the death of the mother or birth defects for infants born of women poisoned in this way (Kang and Pedersen 2017; Russell 1997). Calomel fell out of favor by the 20th century due to its toxic mercury and chloride content. As to the purpose of medicinal bottle remnants in a ritual deposit, the context suggests that these may have been used symbolically for their known curative properties where they aligned with the intent of the spell being used.

3.11 Exotic or Unusual Objects

There are several special finds that were buried in association with the cabins, yards, gardens, fence lines, sheds, or in combination with other materials that raise questions about purposeful placement. Even though they do not fit an established pattern of other ritual or magical deposits in the quarter, the content and the contexts of these suggest that they were not randomly disposed-of materials. They are noted here for future reference in the event that similar deposits are found on the Hume Plantation or elsewhere. None were found in a refuse context, as refuse pits were quite recognizable on the slave street. Additionally, the items were of unusual or rare materials that would have been scarce and more difficult to acquire.

3.11.1 Fossilized Coral

A piece of fossilized coral was in a deposit that included one sherd of colono-ware and four oyster shells; these were buried together in the northeast foundation corner of a shed in the backyard of Cabin 3 (Driver's House), which was adjacent to a garden. Coral was not a common item in the Lowcountry, although fossilized coral has been known to wash up on the beaches around the town of Myrtle Beach. In a contemporary context, coral is sold in shops that specialize in hoodoo materials (Long 2001), but its purpose is commercialized and connection to traditional practices may be challenged. It is allegedly symbolic of water and deities associated with water, which puts it in the category of a protective material in hoodoo practice (Long 2001).

3.11.2 Mirror Pieces

Mirror pieces were included in a ritual deposit with two "X"-crossed nails deposited along the boundary between Cabins 7 and 8. Glass and mirrors were symbolic of portals through which, in African magic practices, the spirits of the ancestors could look and see enemies (Harris and Klemm 2024). Pieces of mirror or glass were often inserted on nkisi figures over the top of the head or the belly wherein the magical materials were placed (Thompson 1981: 129–199; Wyatt et al. 1993).

3.11.3 Doll Arm and Hand

The miniature arm and hand of a doll, made of bisque, approximately 2 centimeters long, and dated to the 19th century (c.1860), was found in the backyard of Cabin 4. This was not included in the original twenty-one ritual deposits list because it appeared to be a stand-alone artifact. It was found not in a refuse pit but near the garden area of the backyard. No other doll parts were found (see Figure 11).

Figure 11 Doll arm/hand.

Source: Photo by the author.

It is worth noting because hand or fist charms were popular among enslaved Africans, who wore them as pendants beneath their clothing (Chireau 2003: 47; Long 2001: 114–115). Often made from repurposed doll parts, they have been found in ritual contexts and among personal items worn on the body at other sites in the American South, such as Hermitage Mansion in Tennessee (Russell 1997: 63–80). The hand symbol is associated with good luck and may also be used to ward off evil, linked to the concept of the "Hand of Fatima," also known as the *hamsa* symbol, from Jewish and Islamic influences (Long 2003: 181; Russell 1997: 66–67).

The concept of the "evil eye," also a Middle Eastern influence, was represented with blue eye-bead(s) worn as jewelry or displayed to ward off bad luck from anyone who might wish you ill with a glance (Long 2003; Pinckney 2003). The blue eye-bead was easily synthesized into traditional African practice and its emphasis on the color blue (see Section 3.4.1). The enslaved were exposed to these magical symbols in both West and Central Africa before they arrived in North America.

It is interesting to note that no other dolls or doll parts were found among any of the other cabins. However, because other identifiable magic deposits were placed in garden contexts in the Hume slave quarter, and because the arm/hand symbol, including the use of old doll parts, has been known among hoodoo practitioners, this deposit is worth noting despite its purpose being undetermined at this time.

3.11.4 Rifle Mechanism

A rifle mechanism was found buried beneath the floor of Cabin 3. An X-ray indicated that the mechanism was broken when it was buried and had been deposited in a post–Civil War timeline. The post-emancipation context suggests that there may have been a ritual meaning to it being buried beneath the cabin floor. This item was not assigned a ritual deposit category due to lack of additional contextual evidence. However, other plantation sites have noted the magical qualities that enslaved peoples regarded iron/metal pieces as having and how they treated them and their disposal differently from usual refuse (Davidson 2015). Iron and metal pieces were most easily acquired in the shape of nails, but other items made of iron or metal were similarly valued. This was discussed in Section 3.6. A rifle mechanism, even broken, may have been perceived as a powerful symbol and its special burial away from the refuse pit would suggest that it was treated differently in a purposeful manner (see Figures 12 and 13).

3.11.5 Iron Stove Face Plate

An iron stove face plate was found buried in the backyard of Cabin 4. Cabins for the enslaved did not include cook stoves; they were required either to cook on an open fire in the yard or in their hearths with limited cooking pots, or to attend the

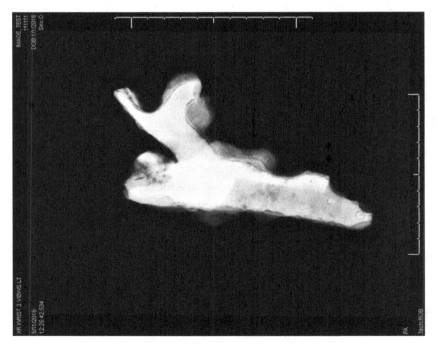

Figure 12 Rifle mechanism X-ray – covered in corrosion.
Source: Author's X-ray.

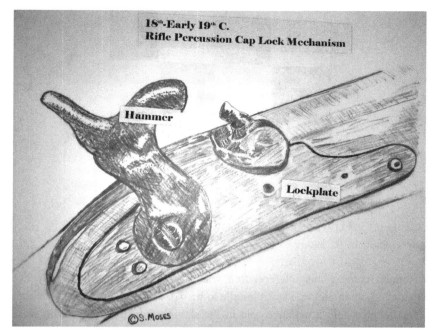

Figure 13 Early 1800s rifle – percussion cap lock illustration.
Source: Illustration by the author.

communal kitchen (on the west side of the slave street – unexcavated) for meals and meal preparation (see the Figure 3 plat map). The face plate was also broken at the time it was buried, also in a post–Civil War period. Like the rifle mechanism, this artifact was not categorized as a ritual deposit, but it did not appear to have had a utilitarian purpose. Due to the magical properties that African groups regarded iron materials as having, it is worth noting here as a possible ritual deposit.

3.11.6 Shark Tooth

A shark's tooth bundled with two nails made up one ritual deposit and the only one of its kind found in the slave quarter (see Figure 14). The tooth was initially thought to belong to a cat, which might suggest a justice or revenge spell. However, closer inspection of the tooth revealed serrated edges; faunal comparisons corrected its identification as a small shark tooth rather than a cat tooth. In hoodoo practice, spells using shark teeth are typically to harness strength and power to dominate others; a shark tooth can thus be thought of as a masculine and aggressive symbol. It was also used in personal adornment as protection against poisonous snakes and bad luck (Rediker 2008). However, in this

Figure 14 Shark tooth from ritual magic deposit.
Source: Photo by the author.

placement context this interpretation was discounted as it was clearly not intended as an amulet or a spirit bundle to be worn by an individual.

Sharks also held a negative role in the slaving industry; slaves who were punished at sea were often thrown to the sharks. Thus, sharks became a symbol of terror and death to the enslaved (Pinckney 2003: 23–24; Rediker 2008). Both the tooth and the nails showed signs of being burned before they were deposited, indicating that a ritual preparation known as altar work was likely.

The deposit itself was not in the context of or in association with a hearth or other burning activities in the cabin; it was placed near the outside of the northeast corner of Cabin 3, the Driver's House. We can infer from this that the deposit was put there surreptitiously by someone not of the driver's household, perhaps as a curse spell to cause harm to the driver and his family. Tensions among the enslaved were not unheard of; shared enslavement did not necessarily mean unity among the enslaved in their shared oppression. This act may indicate a level of jealousy or anger directed at the driver. The nature of this dissention will never be definitively known; it was a personal dispute perhaps, or possibly to do with his relationship with the Main House and the plantation owner providing unequal access to goods not afforded to other enslaved in the quarter.

4 Transformation of the Slave Street Over Time

Prehistoric context suggests temporary Native American campsites, associated lithic maintenance, and local pottery. Levels 5 and lower, 50+ centimeters down, are from a pre-European contact period when Native bands arrived for seasonal hunting and gathering purposes.

Enslaved sedentary living in permanent dwellings can be dated to the pre–Revolutionary War period, or the mid 18th century, by approximate archaeological excavation in Level 4. Remnants of three small dwellings indicate less uniformity along the slave street and possible constructions by the enslaved themselves; smaller tree poles were used for frameworks of residences and boundary fences between the residences. During this time, if there were Natives among the enslaved, they were likely being replaced or had become part of a mixed population of enslaved Africans.

By the early antebellum period, cabin sites excavated in 2015 measured approximately 10 × 12 feet, had become rectangular-shaped, were much more uniform, and had unfinished dirt floors. There are round post stains at the corners that framed simple dwellings.

Construction was based upon local resources and mainly hand-hewn building materials. Archaeological evidence suggests that these constructions and the layout of the slave quarter became much more uniform by the 18th to mid 19th centuries (Vlach 1993).

4.1 Demonstrations of European Power in Landscapes

Excavation levels dating from the late 18th to the early 19th century reveal an architectural shift and use of space, incorporating manufactured hardware and uniform slave cabin construction and placement. Architectural imagery became much more controlled and communicated European power dynamics. Slave streets and the cabins as we have come to envision them were positioned along the drive that led up to the Main House. By this time, any pole roof constructions had been replaced with notched log walls and mortar, called *tabby*, that was made out of crushed oyster shells. Floors continued to be primarily dirt, but uniform hearths and brick chimneys became the norm. Finished floors, larger cabins and hearths, and clapboard siding arrived in the 19th century.

The reasons for the change in the construction style and layout of slave streets have been well debated and reflect an assertion of the European masters' power (Davidson 1971; Ferguson 1992: 63–82; Land 1969; Singleton 2009; Vlach 1993: 13–14; Wells 1998). The visual impact of uniformity within European parameters was purposeful in that it denied the self-expression of enslaved individuals in their lived spaces. Any references to African traditions or beliefs were forced into clandestine practice (Epperson 1999; Singleton 2009).

Despite this mindset, the enslaved were still allowed to utilize their cabin yards for cultivating personal gardens to supplement their subsistence needs and for outdoor tasks. Cooking and other food preparations during hot months were often done outdoors to escape the heat that became stifling indoors. Small sheds that were allowed to store tools and personal belongings freed more space inside the cabins. Pieces of heavy stoneware/salt-glazed jugs were excavated in several backyard contexts, dating to the 18th century, and were likely used to store potable water and other staples within individual cabins for convenience, to be refilled when necessary. The Hume Plantation plat map indicates that there was a well situated in the middle of the slave quarter and in close proximity to the communal kitchen (see Figure 3).

The enslaved found ways to circumvent the slave owners' control of the environment so that they could continue their ritual practices and creation of magic objects and spirit bundles and charms. These practices helped to preserve expressions of identity and beliefs in the face of growing danger and vulnerability for doing so. Mundane and routine tasks observable to the overseer and the plantation owner provided a veil behind which ritual and other illicit practices (such as learning how to read and write) could take place.

The plantation owner's control over the layout of the slave street became a widespread strategy throughout the South by the late 18th century, primarily in relation to slave street orientation and cabin construction (Pogue and Sanford 2020). Prior to that time, most 17th–century accommodation quarters for the enslaved were little more than areas for their habitation or "slave villages." Some plantations provided basic tools and extraneous materials that could be spared for their use, but by and large communities resorted to utilizing building methods they were familiar with from their homelands, such as thatching roofs with bound brush and using poles from young trees to create structural frameworks and fencing.

The only planned construction style for accommodating the enslaved in the 17th century tended to be for those who were *indentured servants* – most of whom were European and in service for a limited time, not under permanent ownership. In the case of indentured servants, accommodations normally consisted of a spare room within the Main House, a small house near the Main House, or a bunkhouse structure where multiple and frequently unrelated people resided (Pogue and Sanford 2020). However, there is no archaeological evidence or historical account of any structure on what became the Hume Plantation grounds that was intended for indentured servants.

By the late 18th and early 19th centuries, specific spatial relationships existed between the Main House and other structures (Vlach 1993). The slave street was not just to accommodate the enslaved; it was meant to showcase the plantation owner's assets, which included his slaves along with livestock and crops. The slave street normally led the visitor through the center of the plantation grounds past the cabins and culminated at the Main House as the pinnacle of the property (Vlach 1993).

Cabin 3 came to be identified as the Driver's House (see Figure 15) and was somewhat larger than the average cabin. The Driver's House measured approximately 6 meters by 5 meters (20 ft × 16 ft). It was identified based upon artifacts associated with equipment for carriage and horse care. The cabin design also set it apart from the other cabins; its unique floor plan showed a wall that split the cabin in half in a north–south orientation instead of the typical east–west split

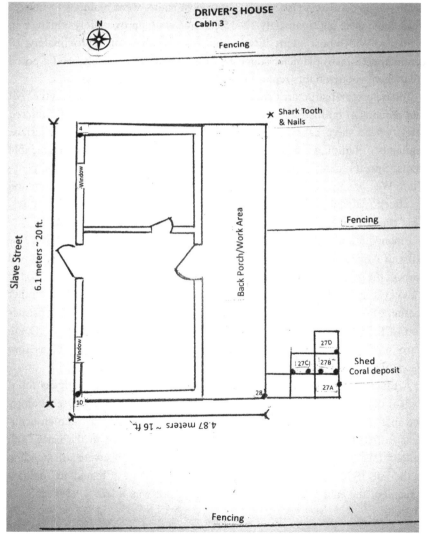

Figure 15 Driver's house – Cabin 3 – floor plan and ritual deposit locations.
Source: Illustration by the author.

otherwise known as "saddlebag" construction (Vlach 1993). This unique split separated the back of the house from the front, or the west side that faced the slave street. It suggests that the back of the house was possibly used by the driver to make or repair tack as part of his duties; he would have been permitted access to some leatherworking tools (awls) to do this job. A saddlebag construction, on the other hand, is intended to split a cabin in half in an east–west orientation to lodge two families.

All of the cabins appeared to have dirt floors and post stains indicating fencing that divided house yards. These post stains were mainly of younger trees; most were approximately 12–15 centimeters (approximately 6 inches) in diameter. Wider post stains in the front of the cabins of approximately 20 centimeter (8 inch) diameter suggest that most of the cabins also had a porch area when wooden floors replaced dirt floors in the 19th century.

Today, original structures from the Hume Plantation no longer survive. All that remains of built structures are surface artifacts such as pieces of scattered brick where slave cabin chimneys and hearths once stood and subsurface remnants of building materials such as nails, hinges, and other nondegradable items. Specific dates of cabin deconstruction are unknown since in the post–Civil War era the face of Cat Island plantations changed. It was common practice to salvage and repurpose building materials for use in other structures. This was true of the slave street cabins as well as the Main House itself.

Emancipation triggered a gradual decline in African population, but a few African Americans stayed on into the early 20th century. Support beams and parts of the gable and roof were repurposed from the Hume Main House into the Yawkey's new lodge construction on South Island in the 1930s, while another section of the original house was relocated and incorporated into the construction of the Main House of the Mount Pleasant Plantation in Andrews, South Carolina belonging to the Fredrick Defoe family. Defoe was appointed as Tom Yawkey's guardian after his parents passed away.[9]

Artifacts excavated on the former Hume slave street provide relative chronological diagnostics based on ceramics, nails, and other materials' technology and manufacture styles and import versus local status. The last known occupancy of the remaining slave cabins can be approximated to the early 20th century (Wells 1998). We know that some of the slave cabins were still standing in the late 1930s because artist Andrew Wyeth visited Cat Island and painted a scene of the cabins in 1937. Wyeth's watercolor was titled "Under the Live Oaks."

---

[9] Nat Ruth, Personal communication re the Hume Plantation salvage/repurposing as a lodge, 2016.

While most of the ritual/magic deposits found were dated to the 18th and 19th centuries, it is notable that six out of twenty-one could be dated to the late 19th and early 20th centuries. This is important in that it demonstrates that hoodoo rituals were still used. Furthermore, evidence suggests that some status materials such as the Victorian faceted amber glass beads were still prized (Davidson 2015).

4.2 Christianity and African Ritual/Magic Traditions

The population ratio of African to European in Georgetown County was estimated at three to one, respectively, in the 18th century.[10] A collection of roughly twenty African slaves organized a group in St. Paul's Parish to stage a revolt known as the Stono Rebellion, or Cato's Rebellion, near Charleston. This event was a mere 60 miles south of the Hume Plantation.

This band of runaways had killed thirty-five people – their plantation owners and other colonists. The runaways targeted any Europeans they encountered as they made their way southward, traveling toward the Florida territory to take advantage of the Spanish promise of freedom to any Africans able to get there.

By 1850, only 10 percent of the population in Georgetown County was European. Whites became very conscious of being the minority population and how vulnerable they were if the enslaved organized rebellion again but with larger, more organized groups. The legal response to contain any future thoughts of rebellion was to institute new regulations on slave punishment and to regulate African spiritual practices. This was particularly prohibitive of religious or spiritual gatherings (Creel 1988: 197–200; Shuler 2009).

Christianizing efforts were scrutinized in the Lowcountry. Despite the misconception that Christian ministers were allowed the freedom to preach anywhere on a traveling circuit, this was not the case (Anderson 2005; Chireau 2003; Creel 1988: 167–210; Pinckney 2003). Traveling ministers had to convince plantation owners to allow them access in the Lowcountry. Sermons and biblical lessons had to promote and justify enslavement to the satisfaction of the plantation owners (Joyner 1984; Pollitzer 2005; Young 2007: 71). Lessons from the King James version that espoused the virtue of obedience of slaves to their masters, that is, Ephesians 6:5–9, were welcomed, as were lessons that promoted conformity, passivity, and submitting to authority. Stories such as Moses' leading the slaves out of Egypt, for example, were met with disapproval. Christianizing the enslaved became more a process born of fear and the need to exert rigid control than of spiritual conversion.

---

[10] See (South Carolina Encyclopedia site) Scencyclopeida.org/sce/entries/African-Americans.

The African Methodist Episcopal church was originally made up of freed and enslaved Africans as a stand-alone church that had broken off to create its own congregation because some white congregants did not want to allow Africans as members in the main church body (Creel 1988). The Yawkey family funded the building of the St. James AME church in the village of Maxwell on Cat Island in 1928 to accommodate descendants of the plantations. It was attended by a traveling minister two Sundays per month and continued for fifty years until the church ended in 1979 (Giauque et al. 2010: 26). Since then, only occasional or commemorative church services are held there once or twice per year.

Despite efforts over two centuries to remove traditional African religious and spiritual beliefs, the converted continued to practice hoodoo and pay respects to various African religions into the 20th century on Cat Island. They saw no fundamental conflict with Christian ideals.

5 Evolution of Lowcountry Hoodoo

Most ritual deposits in the Hume Plantation slave quarter were created during the pre–Civil War era, dating mainly from the early 18th century and pre–Revolutionary War period through the mid 19th century.

Items considered magically charged included iron nails and other metal sources, and water symbols associated with deities and ancestors (shell, coral, blue-colored materials), and were most often considered for their spiritual, protective, curing attributes. Oyster shells at the Hume Plantation were substitutes in place of traditional cowry shells for ritual/magical deposits because cowry shells are not available in the South Carolina Lowcountry. The enslaved also appear to have repurposed European ceramics based upon white or blue colors and occasionally black, and nails for iron content as symbolically power-enhanced materials. Combinations of these items were found in all ritual deposits and create a pattern of ritual and magical practice in the Hume Plantation slave quarter.

Ritual form evolved from Western tribal and Central African (Bakongo) anthropomorphic carved figures (minkisi) that came with the belief systems of the enslaved. Minkisi hollow bellies, in which magical items were placed, became conjure bundles made of cloth/wool sewn with bound items inside to accommodate the need for secrecy and mobility, and the resources that were available. The multitude of nails once driven into minkisi figures to invoke a spirit and infuse power into the spell were now moderately included in multiples of two or four and placed inside the bundle, sometimes bound in the shape of an "X" to replicate the Bakongo cosmogram.

There are clear signs of repurposed Native American pottery, projectile points, and lithics in some of the earlier deposits along the slave street. The enslaved used their own handmade utilitarian pottery pieces (colonoware) sometimes repurposed for ritual deposits. This inclusion of mundane pottery may be attributed to use of colonoware vessels in preparation of ritual objects before depositing them. There is only one instance where an "X" denoting a cosmogram mark may have been purposely etched on a piece of colonoware pottery on the Hume Plantation, though this is not definitive. In comparison, the inclusion of nails or nails bound in an "X" shape within a ritual bundle was more common on this plantation.

The hierarchy of the slave street became clearer over time with the bulk of European hand-me-downs of "luxury" items given to enslaved families concentrated around Cabins 1–4. Cabin 3, the Driver's House, was clearly indicative of an individual whose status among the enslaved had been significantly elevated by the plantation owner. The architecture of the cabin itself is unique for its atypical orientation. Most cabins for the enslaved, if divided, were divided in an east–west orientation, or generally in half, effectively making two cabin spaces out of one, for double occupancy. However, there are no cabins depicted on the plat map that indicate that any other of the original cabins were divided at all, let alone in such an unusual way. Based upon finds of awls, clips, buckles, and other items that could be used in leatherworking, there is speculation that the Driver's House may also have functioned as a workspace to maintain tack and other stable equipment.

Cabin 3 was also the site of most of the ritual deposits (nine out of twenty-one), which suggests that, while the driver and his family may have enjoyed more privileges, they used conjure practices to enhance or protect themselves and their status.

Cabins 5, 6, 7, and 8 were the farthest away from the Main House and excavations produced mainly architectural refuse (nails, hinges, bricks, and mortar) and colonoware, in comparison. Findings may be somewhat skewed due to the difficulty in excavating with more undergrowth and root obstacles than were found in other areas.

No ritual deposits were found beyond Cabin 5 in this lower section of the slave quarter. The assumption is that those less fortunate or who have less than others would turn to hoodoo to improve their lot in life, but if that was so it was not reflected there. Rather, the artifacts and the spartan personal effects suggest a day-to-day focus on survival and maintaining the basics. The individuals living at this end of the quarter were not afforded the same access to resources and privileges and the sparcity of items would not reflect personal choice. It could be that they had little to offer in exchange for a conjurer's assistance. More study about the interpersonal dynamics of a slave street may help to illuminate this difference.

The majority of the spells, based upon the type of ritual deposits found, were for protection and health; spells for prosperity and success were the next most frequently used. Acts of placing ritual deposits in border or "liminal" areas such as fence lines and backyard gardens in stand-alone events suggest an ongoing regard for symbolic materials and the benefits they may hold. These demonstrate that conjure practices and beliefs did not end with emancipation.

While, in the post–Civil War years, many freed Africans migrated away from Cat Island and the Hume Plantation to Charleson and nearby Georgetown or small unincorporated towns, others stayed on Cat Island and continued living in previous slave cabins. A few African Americans immigrated to Cat and South Islands at this time as well.

Emancipated workers earned very little wages in the rice fields during the post–Civil War era and Reconstruction until the crop was no longer an economic mainstay. By the late 19th century, property ownership of the former Hume Plantation had changed hands. Local economy revisited harvesting pine tar and resin for builders and a fishing village sprang up for a time. By the early 20th century, private/elite ownership of the Cat Island property limited its use to a privileged few.

Descendant communities of the enslaved inhabited the newly formed town of Maxwell on Cat Island in the 1920s and the South Island shore fishing village until these could no longer sustain a livelihood. Natural disasters such as hurricanes, flooding, and so on, in addition to economic instability, created yet more challenges. Over time, the population steadily moved back to the mainland for employment and opportunities not available to island living.

Cat, South, and North Islands continue to be utilized as a wildlife and botanical refuge to protect their natural resources and their archaeological sites, and to educate the public about their unique role in Lowcountry history. Most of the residents on the Yawkey Wildlife Center islands today are government employees of the SCDNR and work on the islands' maintenance and preservation programs.

6 Conclusion: Conjure Men and Women Traditions into the 21st Century

6.1 The Three Original Research Questions: Results

At the beginning of the Hume Plantation Slave Street Project, three research questions were posited: (1) What were the hoodoo activities of the enslaved while on their "own time" on the slave street? (2) Can we discern and recognize differences in ritual and magic practices from daily tasks and discard activity in the archaeological record? (3) What hoodoo activities continued in secrecy post-emancipation, or did they revert to practicing openly once the yoke of slavery was removed?

6.1.1 Question 1

Hoodoo activities reflect ongoing concerns with protection, success, and cures or treatments for ailments. There is evidence that suggests disunity or personal grudges between at least two households and spells that were placed in another's space to bring about harm or to sabotage success. There is evidence of a counter spell (black and white ceramic colors used along with crossed nails) indicating that one person was aware that another wished them ill and was trying to safeguard against a vengeful spell. Most African American families relied on their own midwifery and traditional knowledge of plants and curatives for treatment, and hoodoo played an important role in those services as well as spiritual matters. When illness was chronic or other hardships befell a family in terms of personal relationships, economic well-being, mental health, or fertility problems, it was not unusual to turn to both Christian beliefs and prayer and consulting a conjurer. Hoodoo practice is still observed today (Anderson 2005; Creel 1988; Long 2003).

6.1.2 Question 2

Results show that, in relation to hoodoo practices, the enslaved of the Hume Plantation did find ways to enact ritual and magic spells for their needs; these were evident and differentiated in the archaeological record through patterning and symbolism. Materials used and placement jointly suggested activities done in secret, or at least under the cover of daily tasks and mundane activities, whether in daylight or at night, depending upon the prescription of the spell for invoking the spirit, so that the plantation owner and his overseer would not be alerted. The enslaved used the mundane, cast-off, and prehistoric materials at their disposal, which they adapted to their environment. They buttressed their understanding of botanical and marine resources through trial and error and interaction with Native peoples from the earliest periods of enslaved habitation on Cat Island. They learned how to use substitutions for magic objects while still maintaining traditional integrity.

6.1.3 Question 3

Finally, hoodoo activities did continue in the post-emancipation era and were practiced by those freed African Americans who chose to stay. Their descendants continued the traditions of hoodoo, while hoodoo practices continued to evolve as well. While supernatural power is inherent in hoodoo spells, there are indications that social status and concepts of hierarchy had infiltrated into them too. We see a different sort of "power" – the power of social status evidenced over time by increasingly higher-status materials used in the spells (in comparison to the mundane articles, cast-offs, and hand-me-downs that were ubiquitous in the enslaved period). This transition occurred slowly, over decades, and began on the slave street in pre-emancipation times when upper slave street enslaved (those who worked in the Main House or lived closest to it) benefited from access to imported materials – fine china, glassware, and other items not available to all enslaved. Magic deposits into the early 20th century reveal more manufactured metal objects and expensive materials (multifaceted popular culture glass beads, more porcelain – no more earthenware objects). The emphasis appears to shift from natural substances to those items that were commercially produced or more costly. Spells may have been perceived as being more effective with items such as these. However, throughout these changes there is still an acknowledgment of basic supernatural properties being associated with specific objects, colors, materials, and traditional symbolisms.

Hoodoo is still used today for calling upon spirits, saints, and ancestors to help protect, cure, intervene in relationships, enable divination, or create benefits for the individual and/or family (Martin 2012). Hoodoo revenge spells and black magic are also actively practiced. Hoodoo is considered witchcraft when it is used to work against the balance and order of society. However, hoodoo is also considered consistent with Nature in that it has two sides that can be construed as good and bad, respectively, as does Nature. Even when the darker side of hoodoo is practiced, as in "justice" spells – where the person casting the spell is requesting the punishment of someone who has harmed them or their loved one(s) – neither the spell nor the caster is considered evil because the spell is justified. It is perceived as righting a wrong and putting things back into order and balance (Anderson 2005: 134–149; Creel 1988). When harm is intended for personal gain or other selfish reasons, it is witchcraft or black magic.

Conjurers and their skills are passed from one generation to the next within families, developing what they view as natural born skills, depending upon areas of interest and perceived psychic abilities. Conjurers are consulted for spiritual and personal advice; they prepare ritual articles for their clients and instructions on how to use them in exchange for monetary payment or favors that the client can bestow in a barter-like system. Sometimes they do not charge for their services at all (Anderson 2005; Long 2001).

6.2 Funerary Practices and Honoring the Dead

There are two African American cemeteries on Cat Island today: Maxwell cemetery and Sargent cemetery. These served descendant African communities into the 20th century, though neither is active now. They are, rather, the subject of a preservation project, "Listen to the Ancestors" (McGahee and Edmonds 2007). People (tribal descendant populations from West and Central Africa) still visit the gravesites on occasion to honor their ancestors and practice the Bakongo and Gullah traditions of marking the graves to show respect and reverence for the ancestors (McGahee and Edmonds 2007).

Water is still a potent symbol connecting the living world and the spirit world. Many gravesites are decorated with objects associated with water, such as shells, pitchers, bottles, and repurposed jars. These items are ritually broken and left on the grave upside down because it is believed that the ritual breakage helps the spirit escape so that it can move on to the spirit world (McGahee and Edmonds 2007). Other ritual objects include things related to light, such as candle holders and lamp shades – intended to aid the spirit by lighting its way as it moves on (McGahee and Edmonds 2007: 11, 18–19). Finally, personal items that held meaning for the deceased are also occasionally left at the gravesite (McGahee and Edmonds 2007). Visitors are dissuaded from disturbing or cleaning off left objects to avoid disturbing the spirits. One can see decades-old artifacts around gravesites where they are less susceptible to time and decomposition.

6.3 Conjure Today

Ideologically, observing traditional African beliefs and practicing hoodoo while also following Christian teachings is not necessarily considered to be in conflict (Long 2003). Conjurers may belong to the AME Church or to other denominations and simultaneously practice hoodoo as reverence for a creator god and ancestors is regarded as consistent with values that embrace both (Nichols 1989). For instance, keeping holy water and cloths from Catholic services around the house for cleansing as well as protective actions has always been encouraged and demonstrates the synthesis between Christian and African perspectives among followers (Creel 1988; Nichols 1989).

According to descendants, in the 1920s and 1930s there were three known local families in Georgetown and Horry Counties with conjurers among them. Once a year they would drive to New York State from South Carolina to gather in a town outside Albany, New York. These gatherings were much like family reunions, although the families were not necessarily biologically related. They felt joined spiritually through their root men and women. There, they would spend several days sharing community, traditional conjure knowledge, and resources in conjuring practices. In the latter half of the 20th century, many of these generationally taught root men were decreasing in number due to loss of interest among their youth and there was concern about carrying on the traditions. However, in the 21st century there seems to have been a resurgence in interest and more among the new generations are learning these traditions (Pinckney 2003).

6.4 Ritual Crime and Hoodoo in Today's World

Cemeteries today are a locus for hoodoo work. Conjurers will visit cemeteries or send their clientele there to invoke a prepared spell jar, a modern version of a spirit bundle. The author of this Element is an archaeologist with a subspecialty in forensic archaeology used to assist law enforcement in relation to clandestine burials and other outdoor crime scenes, and crime scene analysis. In 2012 the author was called upon by law enforcement to consult on and assist with an investigation into cemetery disturbances where evidence of hoodoo activity was taking place (Moses 2020). There was more than one cemetery involved, but only one requested law enforcement intervention. The belief was that if the motivations were discovered, this might help to identify the perpetrators (Moses 2020). Most of the ritual evidence indicated magic spells intended to address relationship problems, some appeared to be requests for healing, and there was also evidence of revenge spells (Moses 2020).

Selected graves had been partially dug up and spell jars were placed near the coffins. None of the decedents had been disturbed in their coffins. Cemetery maintenance workers would find disturbed graves when they reported for work and the initial response was to collect the items left in and around the graves and fill the graves back in, eliminating all evidence of the disturbance. Several spell jars were thrown away and the gravesites were cleaned of residue candle wax, black feathers, eggs, and empty alcohol bottles or cans as a result (Moses 2020). This was done to protect the reputation of the cemetery and prevent distress for the families of the deceased. It was initially believed that pranksters were perpetrating these activities and that they would eventually lose interest and stop.

However, cemeteries continued to suffer from gravesite disturbances despite management investing in surveillance cameras. The local police were called and patrols increased around the area during nighttime hours. Still, disturbances continued and they could not apprehend the perpetrators. The author was called in to provide some insight into the hoodoo practices and assess the crime scenes.

Spell jars and ritual materials that were not disposed of were analyzed for contents. Spell jars contained varied ingredients including peppers, polaroids (presumably of the intended targets of the spells), eggs, dirt (assumed to be *goopher dirt* – dirt collected from specific graves), black or red ribbons, and pieces of white paper with conjure words of power written on them (Moses 2020). Candle wax (white, red) was present over the lid of some of the jars, suggesting altar work. Headstones or grave markers had coins scattered about the top of the grave; some gravesites also had broken eggs and feathers (white or black) around them (Moses 2020).

The ingredients spoke to the different kinds of spell for different individuals; it appeared that there was no single participant involved in serial acts but that several individuals were each engaging in individual acts, since the spell jars and their contents were very disparate. When the scrutiny of one cemetery became too intense, hoodoo rituals would appear at other cemeteries in the region, followed by a silent period when no activities were detected. When the practices reappeared, they were very sporadic over the following year. It is not known if they stopped altogether or relocated to less risky cemeteries; most cemeteries involved were not eager to share this information. This case is meant only as one example of a collection of hoodoo practices in one place in a modern era; it is not intended to suggest that hoodoo is inherently criminal.

Hoodoo practice takes many forms and of course most do not require the attention of law enforcement. The vast majority of conjure magic is directed at assistance for relationships, health, divination, and success. Hoodoo magic is practiced around the home and in other places where spiritual forces are believed to gather. Black magic spells make up a minority of incidences (Anderson 2005; Chireau 1997).

The conjuring tradition may run in cycles of generational interest and social change, but it is a tradition that is integral to descendant African American identity in the South. Of course, not all subscribe to its efficacy or participate, and in today's world commercialism has entered in to create an economic industry based upon tourism and popular culture appeal, which has added yet another new dimension.

Most would agree that historically hoodoo provided a lifeline of hope and belief through a violent and oppressive chapter in African American history. The ancestors still had a role in the lives of the living who desperately needed to feel tethered to their own culture and the beliefs that were denied them under the oppression of enslavement. Hoodoo cultivated respect for those with know-ledge of Nature and its plants and animals; it influenced and was influenced by multiple cultures to evolve into something new. It provided an outlet for rage, jealousy, and revenge among those who were otherwise left feeling helpless. Today, conjure magic continues to adapt to the needs of its participants and endures as a tradition in the test of time.

References

Anderson, J. E. (2005). *Conjure in African American Society*. Baton Rouge, LA: Louisiana State University Press.

Bassani, E. (1977). Kongo Nail Fetishes from the Chiloango River Area. *African Arts*, 10: 36–40.

Bell, C. (2009). *Ritual Theory, Ritual Practice*. Reprint. Oxford: Oxford University Press.

Blair, E. H., Pendleton, L. S. A. and Francis Jr., P. (2009). *The Beads of St. Catherine's Island*. Anthropological Papers No. 89. New York, NY: American Museum of Natural History.

Bockie, S. (1993). *Death and the Invisible Powers: The World of Kongo Belief*. Bloomington, IN: Indiana University Press.

Butler, N. (2019). Indigo in the Fabric of Early South Carolina. Charleston County Public Library, August 16. www.ccpl.org/charleston-time-machine/indigo-fabric-early-south-carolina (accessed September 19, 2024).

Canopy Family. (2018). Gumbo Limbo Tree: *Bursera simaruba*. Canopy Tower, June 18. https://canopytower.com/gumbo-limbo-tree (accessed September 19, 2024).

Chireau, Y. (1997). Conjure and Christianity in the Nineteenth Century: Religious Elements in African American Magic. *Religion and American Culture: A Journal of Interpretation*, 7(2): 225–246.

Chireau, Y. P. (2003). *Black Magic: Religion and the African Conjuring Tradition*. Berkeley, CA: University of California Press.

Creel, M. W. (1988). *A Peculiar People: Slave Religion and Community-Culture Among the Gullahs*. New York, NY: New York University Press.

Cross, J. R. (1985). *Historic Ramblin's Through Berkeley*. Berkeley County, SC: J. R. Cross.

Cuddy, T. W. and Leone, M. P. (2008). New Africa: Understanding the Americanization of African Descent Groups Through Archaeology. In C. Colwell-Chanthaphonh and T. J. Ferguson (eds.), *Collaboration in Archaeological Practice: Engaging Descendant Communities*, pp. 203–224. Lanham, MD: Altamira Press.

Davidson, C. G. (1971). *The Last Foray: The South Carolina Planters of 1860 – A Sociological Study*. Columbia, SC: University of South Carolina Press.

Davidson, J. M. (2015). A Cluster of Sacred Symbols: Interpreting an Act of Animal Sacrifice at Kingsley Plantation, Fort George Island, Florida (1814–39). *International Journal of Historical Archaeology*, 19: 76–121.

Drewel, H. J. and Mason, J. (1998). Exhibition Preview: Beads, Body and Soul – Art and Light in the Yoruba Universe. *African Arts*, 31(1): 18–35.

Eddins, O. N. (2024). The History of Trade Beads. Peach State Archaeological Society. https://peachstatearchaeologicalsociety.org/artifact-identification/beads/historic-trade-beads/ (accessed September 19, 2024).

Epperson, T. W. (1999). Constructing Differences: The Social and Spatial Order of the Chesapeake Plantation. In T. A. Singleton (ed.), *"I, Too, Am America": Archaeological Studies of African-American Life*, pp. 159–172. Charlottesville, VA: University Press of Virginia.

Ferguson, L. (1992). *Uncommon Ground: Archaeology and Early African America 1650–1800*. Washington, DC: Smithsonian Institution Press.

Ferling, J. (2004). *A Leap in the Dark: The Struggle to Create the American Republic*. Oxford: Oxford University Press.

Fontana, B. L. (1970). Review: Historical Archaeology. Ivor Noel Hume. Alfred A. Knopf, New York, 1969. xiii + 360 pp., 43 figs., index. $10.00. *American Antiquity*, 35(1): 111–112. https://doi.org/10.2307/278189.

Gallay, A. (2002). *The Indian Slave Trade: The Rise of the English Empire in the American South, 1670–1717*. New Haven, CT: Yale University Press.

Giauque, C., Betsworth, J. and Durbetaki, L. (2010). *From Rice Plantations to Baseball Diamonds: The History of the Tom Yawkey Wildlife Center in Georgetown County, South Carolina*. Georgetown, SC: Yawkey Foundation and the Tom Yawkey Wildlife Center.

Gourdin, K. (2023). James Town on Santee. *Berkeley Independent*, March 15.

Gregory, C. A. (1996). Cowries and Conquest: Towards a Subalternate Quality Theory of Money. *Comparative Studies in Society and History*, 38(2): 195–217. English translation.

Haour, A. (2019). Cowries in the Archaeology of West Africa: The Present Picture. *Azania*, 54(3): 287–321.

Harris, S. L. and Klemm, P. (2024). Power Figure (Nkisi Nkondi), Kongo Peoples, https://smarthistory.org/nkisi-nkondi-kongo-people/ (accessed September 19, 2024).

Heath, B. (1999). *The Archaeology of Slave Life at Thomas Jefferson's Poplar Forest*. Charlottesville, VA: University of Virginia Press.

Hogendorn, J. and Johnson, M. (1986). *The Shell Money of the Slave Trade*. Cambridge: Cambridge University Press.

Hyatt, H. (1973). *Hoodoo-Conjuration-Witchcraft-Rootwork*. Vol. 3. St. Louis, MO: Western.

Insoll, T. (2015). *Material Explorations in African Archaeology*. Cambridge: Cambridge University Press.

Jacobs, H. A. (1987). *Incidents in the Life of a Slave Girl: Written by Herself.* Edited by J. F. Yellin. Cambridge, MA: Harvard University Press.

Joseph, J. W. (1989). Pattern and Process in the Plantation Archaeology of the Lowcountry of Georgia and South Carolina. *Historical Archaeology*, 23: 55–68.

Joseph, J. W. (2011). ". . . All of Cross": African Potters, Marks, and Meanings in the Folk Pottery of the Edgefield District, South Carolina. *Historical Archaeology*, 45(2): 134–155.

Joyner, C. (1984). *Down by the Riverside.* Champaign, IL: University of Illinois Press.

Judge, C. and Judge, T. M. (1994). *Archaeological Reconnaissance and Historical Research of the Tom Yawkey Wildlife Center, Georgetown County, South Carolina.* Report. Columbia, SC: Heritage Trust and State of South Carolina Historical Preservation Office, Records Department.

Kang, L. and Pedersen, N. (2017). *Quackery: A Brief History of the Worst Ways to Cure Everything.* New York, NY: Workman.

Klingelhofer, E. (1987). Aspects of Early Afro-American Material Culture: Artifacts from the Slave Quarters at Garrison Plantation, Maryland. *Historical Archaeology*, 21(2): 112–119.

Lachicotte, A. M. (1993). *Georgetown Rice Plantations.* Georgetown, SC: Georgetown County Historical Society.

Land, A. C. (1969). *Bases of the Plantation Society.* Columbia, SC: University of South Carolina Press.

Langley, C. A. (1984). *South Carolina Deed Abstracts 1719–1772.* Vol. II. Easley, SC: Southern Historical Press.

Lapidus, I. (2002). *A History of Islamic Societies*, 2nd ed. Cambridge: Cambridge University Press.

Lauber, A. W. (2002). *Indian Slavery in Colonial Times within the Present Limits of the United States, South Carolina Statutes II*, 201. Reprint of 1913 ed. Forest Grove, OR: University Press of the Pacific.

Lerch, P. B. (2004). *Waccamaw Legacy: Contemporary Indians Fight for Survival.* Tuscaloosa, AL: University of Alabama Press.

Long, C. M. (2001). *Spiritual Merchants: Religion, Magic and Commerce.* Knoxville, TN: University of Tennessee Press.

Marcoux, J. (2012). Glass Trade Beads from the English Colonial Period in the Southeast, ca. A.D. 1607–1783. *Southeastern Archaeology*, 31(2): 157–184.

Marshall, L. W. (2012). Typological and Interpretive Analysis of 19th Century Bead Cache in Coastal Kenya. *Journal of African Archaeology*, 10(2): 189–205.

Martin, K. (2012). *Conjuring Moments in African American Literature: Women, Spirit Work, and Other Such Hoodoo*. New York, NY: Palgrave Macmillan.

Maryland Archaeological Conservation Lab (MACL). (2002). Diagnostic Artifacts in Maryland: Colonial Ceramics. https://apps.jefpat.maryland.gov/ diagnostic/ColonialCeramics/index-colonial.html (accessed September 19, 2024).

McEwan, B. G. (ed.) (2000). *Indians of the Greater Southeast: Historical Archaeology and Ethnohistory*. Gainesville, FL: University of Florida Press and the Society for Historical Archaeology.

MacGaffey, W. (2000). *Kongo Political Culture*. Bloomington, IN: Indiana University Press.

McGahee, S. H. and Edmonds, M. W. (2007). *South Carolina's Historic Cemeteries: A Preservation Handbook*. Columbia, SC: South Carolina Department of Archives and History.

Miller, G. L. (1993). Thoughts Towards a User's Guide to Ceramic Assemblages, Part IV: Some Thoughts on Classification of White Earthenwares. *Council for Northeast Historical Archaeology Newsletter*, 26: 4–7. See pp. 15–22 at https://cneha.org/newsletters/millerguide.pdf (accessed October 9, 2024).

Minges, P. (ed.) (2004). *Black Indian Slave Narratives*. Winston-Salem, NC: John F. Blair.

Mitchell, F. (1999). *Hoodoo Medicine: Gullah Herbal Remedies*. Columbia, SC: Summerhouse Press.

Momodu, S. (2023). Congo Free State (1885–1908). BlackPast, January 20. www.blackpast.org/global-african-history/congo-free-state-1885-1908/ (accessed October 8, 2024).

Moses, S. (2020). Cemetery Hoodoo: Culture, Ritual Crime and Forensic Archaeology. *Forensic Science International: Synergy*, 2: 17–23.

Mullins, P. R., Ylimaunu, T., Brooks, A., Kallio-Seppä, T., Kuorilehto, M., Nurmi, R., Oikarinen, T., Herva, V. P. and Symonds, J. (2013). British Ceramics on the Northern European Periphery: Creamware Marketing in Nineteenth-Century Northern Finland. *International Journal of Historical Archaeology*, 17(4): 632–650.

Murphy, J. M. and Sanford, M. M. (2001). *Osun Across the Waters: A Yoruba Goddess in Africa and the Americas*. Bloomington, IN: Indiana University Press.

Nash, R. C. (2009). Domestic Material Culture and Consumer Demand in the British Atlantic World: Colonial South Carolina 1670–1770. In D. S. Shields (ed.), *Material Culture in Anglo America: Regional Identity and Urbanity in the Tidewater, Lowcountry, and Caribbean*, pp. 221–266. Columbia, SC: University of South Carolina Press.

National Park Service (NPS). (2017). North Carolina, South Carolina, Georgia, Florida: Gullah Geechee Cultural Heritage Corridor. www.nps.gov/articles/gullahgeechee.htm (accessed September 19, 2024).

Nichols, E. (1989). *The Last Miles of the Way: African American Homegoing Traditions, 1890–Present*. Columbia, SC: South Carolina State Museum.

Njoku, O. N. (1991). Magic, Religion and Iron Technology in Precolonial North-Western Igboland. *Journal of Religion in Africa*, 21(3): 194–215.

North Carolina Department of Natural and Cultural Resources (NC-DNCR). (2016). Carolina Charter Issued, 1663. NC-DNCR, March 24. www.dncr.nc.gov/blog/2016/03/24/carolina-charter-issued-1663 (accessed September 19, 2024).

Ogundiran, A. (2002). Of Small Things Remembered: Beads, Cowries, and Cultural Translations of the Atlantic Experience in Yorubaland. *International Journal of African Historical Studies*, 35(2–3): 427–457.

Olson, S. (1963). Dating Early Plain Buttons by Their Form. *American Antiquity*, 284: 551–554.

Opie, I. and Tatum, M. (1989). *A Dictionary of Superstitions*. New York, NY: Oxford University Press.

Parrinder, G. (1969). *West African Religion: A Study of Beliefs and Practices of Akan, Ewe, Yoruba, Ibo, and Kindred Peoples*. London: Epworth Press.

Peck, D. T. (2001). Lucas Vásquez de Ayllón's Doomed Colony of San Miguel de Gualdape. *Georgia Historical Quarterly*, 85(2): 183–198.

Pinckney, R. (2003). *Blue Roots: African-American Folk Magic of the Gullah People*, 2nd ed. Orangeburg, SC: Sandlapper.

Pogue, D. J. and Sanford, D. (2020). Housing for the enslaved in Virginia. *Encyclopedia Virginia*, December 7. https://encyclopediavirginia.org/entries/slave-housing-in-virginia (accessed September 19, 2024).

Polhemus, R. R. (1977). Archaeological Investigation of the Tellico Blockhouse Site (40MR50): A Federal Military and Trade Complex. Unpublished report submitted to the Tennessee Valley Authority.

Pollitzer, W. S. (2005). *The Gullah People and Their African Heritage*. Athens, GA: University of Georgia Press.

Rediker, M. (2008). History from below the Water Line: Sharks and the Atlantic Slave Trade. *Atlantic Studies*, 5(2): 285–297.

Rogers, Jr., G. C. (2002). *The History of Georgetown County, South Carolina*, 6th ed. Spartanburg, SC: Reprint Company.

Rucker, W. C. (2006). *The River Flows On: Black Resistance, Culture, and Identity Formation in Early America*. Baton Rouge, LA: Louisiana State University Press.

Rushing, F. (2011). Bottle Trees Move Beyond Their Roots. *Wall Street Journal*, August 12. www.wsj.com/articles/SB1000142405311190391810457650268 1100923012 (accessed September 19, 2024).

Russell, A. E. (1997). Material Culture and African-American Spirituality at the Hermitage. *Historical Archaeology*, 31(2): 63–80.

Savit, T. L. (1978). *Medicine and Slavery: The Diseases and Health Care of Blacks in Antebellum Virginia*. Urbana, IL: University of Illinois Press.

Sea Grant Consortium (SGC). (2014). Carolina's Gold Coast: The Culture of Rice and Slavery. *Coastal Heritage Magazine*, 28(1). www.scseagrant.org/carolinas-gold-coast-the-culture-of-rice-and-slavery/ (accessed September 12, 2024).

Sharfstein, D. (2007). Crossing the Color Line: Racial Migration and the One-Drop Rule: 1600–1860. *Minnesota Law Review*, 91(3): 592–656.

Sharrer, T. (1971). Indigo in Carolina 1671–1796. *South Carolina Historical Magazine*, 72(2): 94–103.

Shaw, M. (2012). Slave Cloth and Clothing: Craftsmanship, Commerce, and Industry. Museum of Early Southern Decorative Arts. www.mesdajournal .org/2012/slave-cloth (accessed September 19, 2024).

Shepherd, R. E. (2014). Going Up the Country: A Comparison of Elite Ceramic Consumption Patterns in Charleston and the Carolina Frontier. Thesis, University of South Carolina.

Shuler, J. (2009). Negro Acts: Communication and African American Declarations of Independence. In *Calling Out Liberty: The Stono Slave Rebellion and the Universal Struggle for Human Rights*, pp. 98–115. Jackson, MS: University Press of Mississippi.

Singleton, T. A. (ed.) (1999). *"I, Too, Am America": Archaeological Studies of African-American Life*. Charlottesville, VA: University Press of Virginia.

Singleton, T. A. (2009). *The Archaeology of Slavery and Plantation Life*. Walnut Creek, CA: Left Coast Press.

South Carolina Department of Natural Resources (SCDNR). (2022). Tom Yawkey Wildlife Foundation. https://shorturl.at/SuRaD (accessed September 19, 2024).

Stine, L. F., Cabak, M. A. and Groover, M. D. (1996). Blue Beads as African-American Cultural Symbols. *Historical Archaeology*, 30(3): 49–75.

Swanton, J. R. (1946). *The Indians of the Southeastern United States*. Washington, DC: Smithsonian Institution Press.

Thomas, N. W. (1917). Some Ibo Burial Customs. *Journal of the Royal Anthropological Institute of Great Britain and Ireland*, 47: 160–213.

Thompson, R. F. (1981). *The Four Moments of the Sun*. Washington, DC: National Gallery of Art.

Thompson, R. F. (1983). *Flash of the Spirit: African and Afro-American Art and Philosophy*. New York, NY: Random House.

Thomson, W. C. (1846). Narrative of Mr. William Cooper Thomson's Journey from Sierra Leone to Timbo, Capital of Fútah, Jàllo, in Western Africa. *Journal of the Royal Geographical Society of London*, 16: 106–138.

Trinkley, M. (1990). *An Archaeological Context for the South Carolina Woodland Period*. Chicora Foundation Research Series 22. Columbia, SC: South Carolina Department of Archives and History/Chicora Foundation. https://chicora.org/pdfs/RS22%20-%20Woodland%20Context%20compressed.pdf (accessed September 19, 2024).

Vlach, J. M. (1993). *Back of the Big House: The Architecture of Plantation Slavery*. Fred W. Morrison Series in Southern Studies. Chapel Hill, NC: University of North Carolina Press.

Walbert, D. (2008). Colonial North Carolina (1600–1763). NCPedia/Anchor. https://dev.ncpedia.org/anchor/colonial-north-carolina-1600 (accessed September 12, 2024).

Wassie, M. (2021). Color Symbolism in African Culture. *Ethiopian Herald*, June 29.

Wells, T. (1998). Nail Chronology: The Use of Technologically Derived Features. *Historical Archaeology*, 32(2): 78–99.

Wilkie, L. A. (2000). *Creating Freedom: Material Culture and African American Identity at Oakley Plantation, Louisiana, 1840–1950*. Baton Rouge, LA: Louisiana State University Press.

Wood, P. H. (1974). *Black Majority: Negroes in Colonial South Carolina from 1670 through the Stono Rebellion*. New York, NY: W. W. Norton & Company.

Wyatt, M., Harris, M., Williams, S. and Driskell, D. (1993). *Astonishment and Power: The Eyes of Understanding – Kongo Minkisi/The Art of Renee Stout*. Washington, DC: Smithsonian Institution Press.

Young, J. R. (2007). *Rituals of Resistance: African Atlantic Religion in Kongo and the Lowcountry South in the Era of Slavery*. Baton Rouge, LA: Louisiana State University Press.

Zepke, T. (1998). *Lighthouses of the Carolinas: A Short History and Guide*. Sarasota, FL: Pineapple Press.

Acknowledgments

I am grateful to the Northern Arizona University Faculty Grants Project; the Tom Yawkey Wildlife Center, especially Jamie Dozier, the manager; the South Carolina Department of Natural Resources; and the Cambridge University Press peer reviewers for their insights and suggestions.

Cambridge Elements ≡

Magic

William Pooley
University of Bristol

William Pooley is Senior Lecturer in Modern History at the University of Bristol and co-editor of the forthcoming *Cambridge Companion to the Witch*. He is the author of *Body and Tradition in Nineteenth-century France: Félix Arnaudin and the Moorlands of Gascony* (2019) and co-author of the CUP Element *Creative Histories of Witchcraft: France, 1790-1940* (2022). His next book is a history of witchcraft in France from the French Revolution to World War Two.

About the Series

Elements in Magic aims to restore the study of magic, broadly defined, to a central place within culture: one which it occupied for many centuries before being set apart by changing discourses of rationality and meaning. Understood as a continuing and potent force within global civilisation, magical thinking is imaginatively approached here as a cluster of activities, attitudes, beliefs and motivations which include topics such as alchemy, astrology, divination, exorcism, the fantastical, folklore, haunting, supernatural creatures, necromancy, ritual, spirit possession and witchcraft.

Cambridge Elements ≡

Magic